**Book III**

# EARTH SCIENCE ACTIVITIES FOR GRADES 2–8

---

*Science Curriculum Activities Library*

MARVIN N. TOLMAN
JAMES O. MORTON

*illustrated by Carolyn Quinton*

D1385005

*Parker Publishing Company, Inc.*
*West Nyack, New York*

©1986 by
PARKER PUBLISHING COMPANY, INC.
West Nyack, New York

10   9   8

Library of Congress Catalog Card Number: 86-61403

ISBN 0-13-222522-0

Printed in the United States of America

# ABOUT THE AUTHORS

## DR. MARVIN N. TOLMAN

Trained as an educator at Utah State University, Marvin N. Tolman began his career as a teaching principal in rural southeastern Utah. The next eleven years were spent teaching grades one through six in schools of San Juan and Utah Counties and earning graduate degrees.

Currently associate professor of elementary education, Dr. Tolman has been teaching graduate and undergraduate classes at Brigham Young University since 1975. Subject areas of his courses include math methods, science methods, and computer literacy for teachers. He has served as a consultant to school districts, taught workshops in many parts of the United States, and published several articles in professional journals. Dr. Tolman is one of two authors of *What Research Says to the Teacher: The Computer and Education*, published in 1984 by the National Education Association and a coauthor of *Computers in Education*, published by Prentice-Hall, 1986.

Dr. Tolman now lives in Spanish Fork, Utah, with his wife, Judy, and their five children.

## DR. JAMES O. MORTON

For more than 30 years, James O. Morton, Ed.D., Teachers College, Columbia University, has taught students of all ages. He began his career as an elementary school teacher in the Salt Lake City, Utah public schools, where he served later as a principal and as curriculum director. For one year Dr. Morton was a visiting lecturer in education at Queens College, New York City. He also served as an instructor on the summer faculty of Teachers College, Columbia University. For fifteen years Dr. Morton was an associate professor of science education at the University of Utah.

Dr. Morton has served as a national consultant in the development of science curriculum from early childhood through university graduate programs in all geographical areas of the United States. His publications have appeared in scientific and professional journals.

Dr. Morton currently works as a writer and science consultant and lives with his wife, Lornel, in Klamath Falls, Oregon.

# ABOUT THE *LIBRARY*

The *Science Curriculum Activities Library* provides elementary teachers with over 475 science activities that give students hands-on experience in various areas. To be used in conjunction with your regular science texts, the *Library* includes three books, each providing activities exploring a different field:

- Life Sciences
- Physical Sciences
- Earth Sciences

In most public schools today, emphasis is on the fundamental skills of language arts and mathematics. The teaching of science has often been relegated to a supplementary place in the curriculum. What may be overlooked is that a strong science program with a discovery/inquiry approach can enrich the development of mathematics, as well as other academic content areas. The activities in the *Library* develop these skills. Most activities call for verbal responses, with questions that encourage analyzing, synthesizing, and inferring instead of answering yes or no.

Development of thinking and reasoning skills, in addition to learning content, are the main goals of the *Library*'s science activities. Learning how to learn and how to apply the various tools of learning are more useful in a person's life than is the acquisition of large numbers of scientific facts. Through these process skills, students are encouraged to explore, invent, and create. The learning of scientific facts is a byproduct of this effort, and increased insight and retention associated with facts learned are virtually assured.

# HOW TO USE BOOK III: EARTH SCIENCES

Book III consists of over 160 easy-to-use, hands-on activities in the following areas of earth sciences:

- Air
- Water
- Weather
- The Earth
- Ecology
- Above the Earth
- Beyond the Earth

## Teacher Qualifications

You need not be a scientist to conduct an effective and exciting science program at the elementary level. Interest, creativity, enthusiasm, and willingness to get involved and try something new will go a long way. Two of the most critical qualities of the elementary teacher as a scientist are (1) commitment to helping students acquire learning skills and (2) recognition of the value of science and its implications for the acquisition of such skills.

## Capitalize on Interest

It is expected that some areas will be of greater interest to both you and your students, so these interests should be considered when you select science topics. Since these materials are both nongraded and nonsequential, areas of greatest interest and need can be emphasized. As you gain experience with using the activities, your skill in guiding students toward appropriate discoveries and insights will increase.

## Organizing for an Activity-centered Approach

Trends of the past have encouraged teachers to modify a traditional textbook approach by using an activity-based program, supplemented by the use of textbooks and other materials. We favor this approach, so the following activities encourage hands-on discovery. Valuable learning skills are developed through this direct experience.

One of the advantages of this approach is the elimination of the need for every student to have the same book at the same time, freeing a substantial portion of the textbook money for purchasing a variety of materials and references, including other textbooks, trade books, audio and video tapes, models, and other visuals. References should be acquired that lend themselves developmentally to a variety of approaches, subject matter emphases, and levels of reading difficulty.

## Starter Ideas

Section 1, "Starter Ideas," should be used first. The sequence of other sections may be adjusted according to interest, availability of materials, time of year, or other factors. Some sections use concepts developed in other parts of the book. When this occurs, the activities are cross-referenced so concepts can be drawn from other sections as needed.

Starter Ideas are placed at the beginning of the book to achieve several specific goals:

- To assist in selecting topics for study.
- To provide a wide variety of interesting and exciting hands-on activities from many areas of science. As students investigate these Starter Ideas, they should be motivated to try additional activities in related sections of the book.
- To introduce teachers and students to the discovery/inquiry approach. Having experienced several of these activities, they will spend time on the other sections more efficiently.
- To be used for those occasions when only a short period of time is available and a high-interest independent activity is needed.

## Unique Features

The following points should be kept in mind while using this book:

1. It places the student in the center of the discovery/inquiry approach to hands-on learning.
2. The main goals are problem solving and the development of critical-thinking skills. Content is a spinoff, but is possibly learned with greater insight and meaning than if it were the main objective.
3. It attempts to prepare teachers for inquiry-based instruction and sharpen their guidance and questioning techniques.
4. Most materials recommended for use are readily available in the school or at home.
5. Activities are intended to be open and flexible and encourage the extension of skills through the use of as many outside resources as possible: (a) The use of parents, aides, and resource people of all kinds is recommended throughout; (b) the library, media center and other school resources, as well as a classroom reading center related to the area of study, are essential in teaching most of the sections; and (c) educational television programs and videocassette recorders can often enrich the science program.
6. With the exception of the activities labeled "teacher demonstration" or "whole-class activity," students are encouraged to work individually, in pairs, or in small groups. The teacher gathers and organizes the materials, arranges the learning setting, and serves as a resource person. In many instances, the materials listed on an index card with the

procedure are all students will need in order to perform the activities. Ideas are given in "To the Teacher" at the beginning of each section and in "Teacher Information" at the end of each activity to help you develop your content background and your questioning and guidance skills.

7. Full-page activity sheets, such as "Observation Chart" and "Do You Know This about the Moon?" are offered throughout the book. These sheets can easily be reproduced and kept on hand.

At the end of the book are a bibliography, sources of free and inexpensive materials, and a list of science supply houses. This information will help you organize your program so that each activity is used to its fullest potential.

## Format of Activities

Each activity in this book includes the following information:

- *Activity Number*: Activities are numbered sequentially throughout the book for easy reference.
- *Activity Title*: The title of each activity is in the form of a question that can be answered by completing the activity and that requires more than a simple yes or no answer.
- *Special Instructions*: Some activities are intended to be used as teacher demonstrations or whole-group activities, or require close supervision for safety reasons, so these special instructions are noted.
- *Materials*: Each activity lists the materials needed. The materials used are easily acquired, but, when necessary, special instructions or sources have been given.
- *Procedure*: The steps for the students to follow are given in easy-to-understand language.
- *Teacher Instructions*: Suggested teaching tips and background information follow the procedure. This information supplements that given in "To the Teacher."

## Use of Metric Measures

Most linear measures used are given in metric units followed by standard units in parentheses. This is done to encourage use of the metric system. Other measures, such as capacity, are given in standard units.

## Grade Level

The activities in this book are intended to be nongraded. Many activities in each section can be adapted for use with young children, yet most sections provide challenge for the more talented in the middle and upper elementary grades.

## Final Note

Remember, the discovery/inquiry approach used in *Earth Sciences* emphasizes verbal responses and discussion. With the exception of recording results, activities do not require extensive writing. Discovering the excitement of science and developing new techniques for critical thinking and problem solving should be the major goals of your science program.

*Marvin N. Tolman*
*James O. Morton*

# ACKNOWLEDGMENTS

Mentioning the names of all individuals who contributed to the *Elementary Science Activities Library* would require an additional volume. The authors are greatly indebted to the following:

- Teams of graduate students at the University of Utah for initial assistance and testing of design and methodology.
- Teachers and students of all levels, from early childhood through post doctoral, who taught us while they thought we were teaching them.
- School districts throughout the United States who cooperated by supporting and evaluating ideas and methods used in this book.
- Special consultants who made significant contributions to the development, quality, and accuracy of the manuscript: Lornel T. Morton, Klamath Falls, Oregon (illustrating, typing, and editing); Sue P. Grinvalds, Klamath Falls, Oregon (illustrating); Gregory L. Tolman, Spanish Fork, Utah (illustrating); Bonnie R. Newman, Salt Lake City, Utah (consultant); Kathryn L. J. Ardt, Klamath Falls, Oregon (consultant); Vera A. Christensen, Logan, Utah (media); and Denise Swift (typing)
- Dr. James E. Baird, chairman of the Department of Elementary Education at Brigham Young University, for his encouragement and support, and for running interference to protect precious writing time.
- Finally, the last names of the authors, Tolman and Morton, are correct. However, the first names could well be changed to Judy and Lornel, for without their love, support, encouragement, patience, and acceptance these books could not have been written.

# CONTENTS

## Section 4 WEATHER.................................... 77

## Section 5 THE EARTH .................................. 115

## Section 8 BEYOND THE EARTH . . . . . . . . . . . . . . . . . . . . . . . . . 229

# CONCEPTS/SKILLS INDEX
# FOR BOOK III: EARTH SCIENCES

The following concepts/skills index represents the scientific concepts or "Big Ideas" included in this book. The recommended age or grade levels at which the Big Ideas are introduced or developed in greater depth in each section are broken down this way:

preK: ages 3–5 (early childhood)
K–3: ages 5–8 (kindergarten-primary)
4–8: ages 9–14 (upper grades)

Each concept has been stated in simple but scientifically accurate terms followed by the numbers of recommended activities that introduce or reinforce the concept.

In some sections, background concepts necessary to an understanding of observed behavior cannot be "discovered" by hands-on experiences or activities at the elementary school level. When these Big Ideas are introduced, the activity column of the index will list "Teacher-student/demonstration/discussion." In these situations, strategies for presenting the necessary background information will be found in "To the Teacher" at the beginning of the section and "Teacher Information" after each activity.

As worded, the concepts/skills in this index are intended for teacher use to give an overview of each section. They are *not* intended to be used as an evaluation of student knowledge.

Throughout the book, a hands-on, activity-centered approach is emphasized. The scientific process skills of observing, classifying, communicating, measuring, inferring, and experimenting are intended to be the major outcomes of this program. Content acquisition and development in science and other subject areas will be major concomitant learning. In attempting to recommend age or grade levels at which concepts should be introduced, we recognize that a great variation will exist due to individual differences in students, which only you can determine.

Remember, a positive attitude toward science and "sciencing" on the part of both teachers and students is the major purpose of this book and will determine its effectiveness.

## AIR

| Big Idea | Suggested Grade Level | Activities |
|---|---|---|
| Air is real. Air occupies space. You cannot see it, taste it, or smell it. You can feel it and hear it only when it is moving (wind). | preK–8 | 24, 25 |

# WATER

| Big Idea | Suggested Grade Level | Activities |
|---|---|---|
| We are covered by a deep ocean of air. Our ocean of air extends several miles above the surface of the earth. | 4–8 | Teacher-student/ demonstration/ discussion |
| Air has weight. The weight exerts pressure. | K–8 | 27, 33 |
| Air has pressure. Air pressure pushes in all directions. | 4–8 | 28, 29, 30, 31, 32 |
| Warm air rises. | K–8 | 34, 35 |
| Warm air expands. | 4–8 | 36 |
| Cold air contracts. Cold air is heavier than warm air and usually sinks below (beneath) it. | K–8 | 37, 38, 39 |
| Air can be compressed. | 4–8 | 40, 41 |
| Most air has tiny particles of water in it, called vapor. | K–8 | 42, 43 |
| Water vapor condenses out of cool air. | K–8 | 42, 43 |
| Unless air is saturated, water can evaporate into it. As the temperature of air increases, so does its capacity to contain moisture. | preK–8 | 44 |
| When air is cooled, it gives up water vapor through condensation. | preK–8 | 45, 46, 47 |
| Water has pressure. As depth increases, pressure increases. | K–8 | 50 |
| Surface tension exists because water molecules are attracted to each other. | K–8 | 51, 52, 53 |
| As light travels through water, its speed is reduced. When light enters water at an angle, it is bent or refracted. | K–8 | 54, 55, 56, 57 |
| Pure water has a specific density. The density of water increases as other materials are dissolved in it. | 4–8 | 58, 59 |
| When water is heated, the molecules move more rapidly and the volume increases. | K–8 | 60, 61 |
| Water contracts as it gets colder, but unlike other substances, it expands just a little above freezing point (4°C). | 4–8 | 62 |

## WATER (continued)

| Big Idea | Suggested Grade Level | Activities |
|---|---|---|
| The attraction of unlike substances to each other is called adhesion. Because of adhesion, water molecules tend to climb the sides of a glass. We call this capillary action. (Some other liquids behave similarly. When a blood sample is taken with a capillary tube, capillary action draws blood up the tiny opening in the tube, even against the force of gravity.) | K–8 | 63 |

## WEATHER

| Big Idea | Suggested Grade Level | Activities |
|---|---|---|
| Wind is moving air. | preK–8 | 24 ,25 |
| We can make instruments to measure air temperature, air pressure, moisture in the air (humidity), wind direction, and wind speed. | K–8 | 64, 65, 66, 67, 68, 69, 70, 71, 72, 73, 74 |
| We can use our instruments to help forecast weather. | K–8 | 75 |
| Professional weather forecasters use very sensitive instruments, plus the modern technology of radio, television, and satellites, to study, report, and forecast weather conditions. | K–8 | 76 |
| Traditions, beliefs, superstitions, and history are used by some people to forecast weather. | K–8 | 76 |
| Weather forecasts using any known method are incorrect some of the time. | K–8 | Teacher-student/ demonstration/ discussion |
| Fast-moving air (wind) has lower air pressure. | K–8 | 18 |
| When warm, moist air is cooled, it gives up moisture through condensation (clouds, rain). | K–8 | 43, 80 |
| Large masses of air form under different conditions all over the earth. | 4–8 | 78, 80 |

## WEATHER (continued)

| Big Idea | Suggested Grade Level | Activities |
|---|---|---|
| Warm air masses with high air pressures are called highs and usually bring fair weather. | 4–8 | 78, 80 |
| Cold air masses with higher winds and lower pressures are called love. | 4–8 | 78, 80 |
| When the fronts of different systems come together, the weather in the area is disturbed and changes. | 4–8 | 81 |
| Cold fronts usually bring storms and cooler temperatures. | 4–8 | 81 |
| The currents of large warm bodies of water (oceans, gulfs, etc.) influence or control weather conditions most of the time. | 4–8 | 80, 81 |

## THE EARTH

| Big Idea | Suggested Grade Level | Activities |
|---|---|---|
| A map is a drawing or picture that shows size and/or distance of a real object. | K–8 | 82 |
| Greater distances and larger objects can be shown by changing the scale. | K–8 | 83 |
| High and low places (dimensions) can be shown on a flat map. | K–8 | 84 |
| Shapes of high and low spots can be shown with contour lines on flat maps. | 4–8 | 85 |
| Contour lines can tell us how high and low elevations are on a flat map. | 4–8 | 86, 87 |
| Because the earth is round, a flat map cannot accurately show all the surface of the earth. | 4–8 | 88 |
| The earth's surface (mountains, oceans, etc.) affects the temperature in different parts of the world. | 4–8 | 89, 90 |
| Mountains often affect yearly rainfall. | 4–8 | 90 |

# THE EARTH (continued)

| Big Idea | Suggested Grade Level | Activities |
|---|---|---|
| The earth's crust is shifting and changing. | 4–8 | 91 |
| Earth is a living, changing planet. | K–8 | 92 |
| Water erosion changes the earth's surface. | K–8 | 93 |
| Earthquakes and some other changes in the surface are caused by movements in the earth's crust. | K–8 | 94 |
| Volcanoes are caused when very hot materials from beneath the earth's crust are forced to the surface. | K–8 | 95 |
| Glaciers are formed when snow and rocks are compacted to form ice. | K–8 | 96 |
| Materials settle to the bottom of a body of water according to their size and weight. | K–8 | 97 |
| Rocks are classified in many ways. | 4–8 | 98, 99, 100, 101, 102, 103 |
| Some rocks will dissolve in water. | 4–8 | 104 |
| Crystals can be seen in many rocks. | 4–8 | 105 |
| Each mineral forms a uniquely shaped crystal. | 4–8 | 106 |
| Conglomerates are made up of many rocks glued together. | 4–8 | 107 |
| You can make your own rock collection. | K–8 | 98, 99, 100, 101, 102, 103, 108, 109, 111 |
| Fossils are rock imprints of ancient animals and plants. | K–8 | 110 |
| You can learn many things from a square meter of soil. | 4–8 | 112 |
| Soil is made of finely ground rocks and organic material. | K–8 | 113 |

# ECOLOGY

| Big Idea | Suggested Grade Level | Activities |
|---|---|---|
| A simple plant and animal community is composed of at least six important elements: energy from the sun; air; moisture; soil; plants and scavengers (worms, insects, etc.); and decomposers (bacteria and fungi) to make the soil rich. | K–8 | 114 |
| Plants of many kinds grow above the ground. | K–8 | 114 |
| Plants depend on the sun, air, moisture, and rich soil. | K–8 | 114 |
| Plants release oxygen and moisture into the air. | K–8 | 114 |
| Many plants use energy from the sun, moisture, and rich soil to produce food. They are called primary producers. | K–8 | 114 |
| When all elements function together successfully, it is called a community. | K–8 | 114 |
| Animals do not produce food; they consume it. They are called consumers. | K–8 | 115 |
| Animals that eat plants are called primary consumers. | K–8 | 116 |
| Animals that eat animals are called secondary consumers. | K–8 | 116 |
| Most plant and animal communities are producers, primary consumers, and secondary consumers. | K–8 | 117 |
| When all elements in a community function together in an interdependent way, the community is called an ecosystem. | K–8 | 117 |
| Energy from the sun is the basis of all life and is transferred through the ecosystem in a food chain. | 4–8 | 118 |

| Big Idea | Suggested Grade Level | Activities |
|---|---|---|
| A food web is a more complex way to study an ecosystem. It involves variables (chance and change) in the ecosystem. | 4–8 | 118 |
| Food webs are made up of many food chains. | 4–8 | 118 |
| When people, as secondary consumers, are added to an ecosystem, changes begin to occur. | 4–8 | 119 |
| When one element in the ecosystem changes, often the entire system will change or disappear. | 4–8 | 119 |
| With planning, people can preserve, modify, conserve, and restore natural ecosystems. | 4–8 | 119 |
| You can use the model of an ecosystem to help understand yourself and the environment in which you live. | K–8 | 120 |
| Family and home are very important in your ecosystem. You can help keep them in balance. | K–8 | 121 |
| The school classroom is an important chain in your ecosystem. You can help keep it in balance. | K–8 | 122 |
| You can study your school community as a large ecosystem. | K–8 | 123 |
| There are ways you can help improve all your personal communities and help them function as balanced ecosystems. | K–8 | 124 |
| There are ways to help improve our environment beyond the home and school: | K–8 | 125 |
|    a. Help reduce loud noise. | K–8 | 127 |
|    b. Assist in cleaning up littered areas. | K–8 | 128 |
|    c. Avoid personal littering. | K–8 | 128 |
|    d. Encourage others to avoid littering. | K–8 | 129 |
|    e. Study ways to reduce waste in foods and packaging. | K–8 | 130 |

## ECOLOGY (continued)

| Big Idea | Suggested Grade Level | Activities |
|---|---|---|
| f. Conserve and use your personal resources wisely (food, clothing, books, toys, etc.). | K–8 | 132 |
| Some materials can be recovered and used again. This is called recycling. | 4–8 | 133 |
| Some materials will decay or decompose and return to the food chain. Some (especially plastics) will not. | K–8 | 134 |
| Large communities often improve the environment and reduce pollution with water treatment and sewage disposal plants. | K–8 | 135 |
| Older members of the community can help you learn about the changes that have happened right where you live. | K–8 | 131, 136 |

## ABOVE THE EARTH

| Big Idea | Suggested Grade Level | Activities |
|---|---|---|
| Man has spent many centuries learning to fly. | K–8 | 137 |
| Moving air has less pressure. | 4–8 | 139 |
| Air moving over a curved surface lowers the pressure above it and causes lift. | 4–8 | 139, 140, 141 |
| Airplanes are turned by one or more movable upright fins called rudders. | 4–8 | 140, 141, 142, 143, 144 |
| Elevators located at the rear of the airplane are horizontal movable fins that force the tail up and down to control upward and downward movement. | 4–8 | 140, 141, 142, 143, 144 |
| Ailerons, located at the rear of the wings, are raised and lowered to cause the airplane to tilt or bank. | 4–8 | 140, 141, 142, 143, 144, 145, 146 |
| An action in one direction will cause a reaction in the opposite direction. Newton's third law of motion states: "For every action there is an equal and opposite reaction." | K–8 | 147, 148, 149, 150, 151, 152 |

| Big Idea | Suggested Grade Level | Activities |
|---|---|---|
| Gravity is the attraction of one mass for another. | 4–8 | 153 |
| Excluding air friction, objects fall at the same rate regardless of mass, size, or shape. | K–8 | 153 |
| Inertia is the internal resistance of mass to changing its condition in relation to movement. Newton's first law of motion states that objects at rest remain at rest; objects in motion remain in motion unless acted upon by an outside force. | 4–8 | 154, 155 |
| As masses move apart, the force of gravity falls away rapidly and weightlessness occurs. | K–8 | 156 |
| The sensation of weightlessness in people can be caused by many phenomena. | K–8 | 156 |
| Special terms in this section are used in the following manner: | 4–8 | |

a. *Balloon*—lighter-than-air craft, usually qualified by the means of displacement; for example, hot air, helium, hydrogen.

b. *Glider*—unpowered craft with wings to provide lift.

c. *Airplane*—powered craft with wings and controls for turning.

d. *Jets*—action-reaction engines that depend on an external oxygen supply (air) as part of their combustion; limited to flight in the earth's atmosphere.

e. *Rockets*—action-reaction engines that carry their own oxygen and other fuel components in liquid or solid form.

f. *Aircraft*—a general term referring to any man-made device for flying.

# BEYOND THE EARTH

| Big Idea | Suggested Grade Level | Activities |
|---|---|---|
| Earth is a round, brightly colored globe with continents, oceans, and clouds clearly visible from space. | preK–8 | 157 |
| The earth rotates on its axis once in approximately 24 hours. | K–8 | 158 |
| The earth revolves around the sun once in approximately 365 ¼ days. | 4–8 | 159 |
| The 23½° tilt of the earth remains constant during its revolution, thereby causing seasonal changes. | 4–8 | 159 |
| The earth and other planets revolve around the sun in paths called orbits. | 4–8 | 160 |
| Orbits of planets are not round, but in elongated paths called ellipses. | 4–8 | 160, 162 |
| A smaller object in orbit around a larger object is called a satellite. Man-made satellites are used for many purposes. | 4–8 | 164 |
| The moon is a natural satellite of earth. | 4–8 | 162 |
| There are many facts known about the moon. | 4–8 | 163, 164, 165 |
| Eclipses are caused when the paths of the moon or earth block out direct or indirect light from the sun. | 4–8 | 166 |
| The solar system consists of the sun and other objects kept in orbit around it due to gravitational attraction. | 4–8 | 167 |
| The planets are very different in their mass (size), temperature, and distance from the sun. | 4–8 | 168 |
| There are great differences in size of the planets and in distances between the various planets and the sun. | 4–8 | 169, 170 |
| There are other bodies, such as comets, asteroids and meteors, in orbits and traveling from outer space through the solar system. | 4–8 | 171 |

# Section 1

---

# STARTER IDEAS

# TO THE TEACHER

The following section is a challenge to you. The ideas presented here have been collected over a period of many years from the bright, creative minds of thousands of scientists, teachers, students, and children of all ages. Within your mind are creative ideas we hope these Starter Ideas will stimulate. The challenge is an invitation to explore, inquire, invent, and create.

In these simple, easy, inexpensive activities you will find your special invitation for creative inquiry. With few exceptions, the sections of this book do not build in a sequential way, so you can begin almost anywhere and explore forward or backward.

Starter Ideas are single-concept ideas that range far and wide in the unlimited areas we often try to cover in science. (One dictionary definition of *cover* is *to conceal*. We hope you will not try to conceal these ideas, but instead will uncover, explore, and develop them.) Starter Ideas are intended to start your exploration in the exciting world of the sciences.

Try the ideas at random. When you find something you and your students like, there will usually be a reference to the section of the book where you can explore it in greater depth. If you or your students become bored or don't like an area, think of ways to add interest or move to another science topic. You need not feel you must do everything just because you enjoy something about it. As educators, we know young people do best the things they enjoy most. Your best teaching is done for the same reason. If you find something you don't understand, look for new creative ways to learn and develop the concept. New interests will blossom as you explore new horizons and student interest is likely to increase along with yours.

If there is one "must" everyone in our society needs to understand, it is that we have unlimited wants and limited fragile natural resources. It is important that we use what we have wisely. We must also understand that science, especially the new technology, must remain our servant, not become our master.

Whatever you choose, an activity is in "Starter Ideas" to help you get started. The purpose is to explore and inquire creatively, and through these explorations, to develop every facet of your student's ability to learn.

In this section there is really nothing you have to do but explore, enjoy, and create. Somewhere in the next few pages you will find the place to begin your exciting journey in science.

There is an ancient Chinese saying: "A journey of a thousand miles begins with a single step." It is our hope that Starter Ideas will provide that first step.

# ACTIVITY 1: What Can Air Do to an Egg?

(Teacher demonstration or supervised activity)

## MATERIALS NEEDED

- Hard-boiled egg, peeled
- Glass milk bottle
- Kitchen matches

## PROCEDURE

1. Stick two kitchen matches in the pointed end of the egg.
2. Holding the bottle upside down, light the matches and put the egg into the mouth of the bottle, pointed end first. Hold the egg lightly against the mouth of the bottle—don't push! Keep the bottle upside down.
3. What happened? What can you say about this?

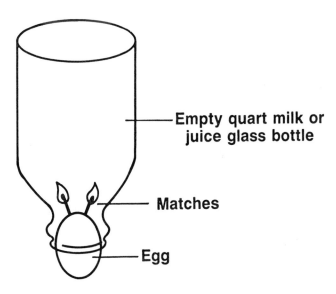

Empty quart milk or juice glass bottle

Matches

Egg

FIGURE 1-1. Bottle with egg and matches.

## TEACHER INFORMATION

The lit matches in the pointed end of the egg will heat the air inside the bottle, causing it to expand. When this happens, warm air is forced out of the bottle (don't push the egg into the top of the bottle or the air can't get out). Soon the matches will go out and the air inside the bottle will cool and contract leaving less pressure inside the bottle than out. When this happens the outside air pressure will force the egg into the bottle.

If the egg is not broken, you can get it out of the bottle by reversing the process. Hold the bottle above your head with the pointed end of the egg in the bottle's mouth. Blow very hard into the bottle. The blowing will increase the air pressure inside the bottle and often push the egg out. If the egg comes only part way out, try pouring warm water on the bottle. The air inside will expand and force the egg out.

The mouth of the bottle should be somewhat smaller (5 mm or ¼) in. in diameter than the egg. If the old-style milk bottle is not available, two-quart or two-liter juice bottles will be about right if you use large eggs. Pullet eggs could be used with bottles having a smaller opening.

# ACTIVITY 2: How Can Air Pressure Make Things Stronger?

## *MATERIALS NEEDED*

- Paper straws
- Raw potato

## *PROCEDURE*

1. Hold a straw near one end and try to stick the other end in a potato. What happened?
2. Place your finger over the top of the straw and stick the other end into the potato (do it fast and hard). What happened?
3. What can you say about this?

## *TEACHER INFORMATION*

When you try to stick the straw with both ends open in the potato, the straw will bend. When you place your finger over the upper end of the straw, the air is trapped inside and the column is strengthened. The straw will go into the potato. (Be sure to stab rapidly and hold the straw near the top during all parts of the activity.)

This may also be found as Activity 31 in Section 2, "Air."

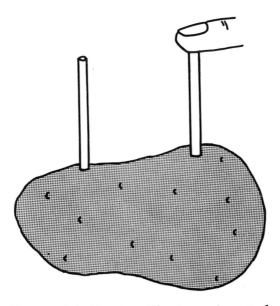

FIGURE 2-1. Potato with straws inserted.

# ACTIVITY 3: What Can a Card Teach You About Air?

(Do this over the sink please!)

## MATERIALS NEEDED

- Water glass
- 5″ × 8″ index card
- Water

## PROCEDURE

1. Fill the glass with water until level with, or a little below, the top
2. Put the index card over the top of the glass.
3. Hold the card in one hand and the glass in the other.
4. Turn the glass upside down and carefully remove your hand from the card.
5. Turn the glass right side up (don't touch the card).
6. What happened. What can you say about this?

## TEACHER INFORMATION

When the glass full of water is turned upside down and the hand removed, the card will stay on the glass and the water will not come out. This is because the pressure of the air pushing on the card is great enough to hold the water in. You can also demonstrate that air pushes in all directions by slowly turning the glass right side up and down again without touching the card.

Be certain the rim of the glass is smooth, without cracks or chips.

# ACTIVITY 4: How Can You Test to See If Air Is in Something?

## MATERIALS NEEDED

- 8-ounce plastic tumbler
- Facial tissue
- Deep bowl filled with water

## PROCEDURE

1. Look at the glass. What is in it?
2. Crumple the tissue and put it in the bottom of the glass.
3. Turn the glass over (be sure the tissue does not fall out) and push it, mouth first, into a deep bowl of water.
4. Now remove the glass without tipping it.
5. What happened to the tissue?
6. What can you say about this?

FIGURE 4-1. Bowl of water with inverted cup at bottom.

## TEACHER INFORMATION

When the glass is lowered mouth first into the bowl of water, the air will be trapped inside and prevent water from entering the glass. Thus, the tissue will remain dry.

This investigation may also be found in Activity 24 in Section 2, "Air."

# ACTIVITY 5:  How Hard Can Air Push?

(Teacher-supervised activity)

## MATERIALS NEEDED

- Clean duplicating fluid can
- Hot plate
- One cup of water

## PROCEDURE

1. Put about one cup of water in a clean duplicating fluid can.
2. Boil the water *with the lid off.*
3. Remove the can from the stove and immediately put the lid on tightly.
4. Observe what happens to the can.

## TEACHER INFORMATION

The steam and expansion of the hot air will force most of the air from the can. When the lid is put on tightly, no air can get back in the can. As the water vapor condenses and the remaining air inside the can cools and contracts, it will create a partial vacuum. The air pressure outside the can will become much greater than the air inside and will gradually crush the can.

# ACTIVITY 6: What Is Another Way to Feel Air Pressure?

## *MATERIALS NEEDED*

- Two suction-cup plungers
- Water

## *PROCEDURE*

1. Moisten the edges of the two plungers. Find a friend.
2. Push the ends of both plungers together. Now pull them apart.
3. What happened?
4. What can you say about this?

## *TEACHER INFORMATION*

When the plungers are pushed together, much of the air between them is forced out, creating a partial vacuum. The outside air pressure keeps them together. Plungers will not work on the moon because there is practically no air pressure.

This demonstration may also be found as Activity 30 in Section 2, "Air."

# ACTIVITY 7: How Can Air Be Compressed?

## *MATERIALS NEEDED*

- Clear plastic 16-ounce shampoo bottle filled with water
- Medicine dropper filled with a small amount of water

## *PROCEDURE*

1. Observe the medicine dropper in the bottle.
2. Gently squeeze the bottle.
3. What happened? What can you say about this?

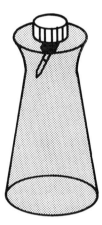

FIGURE 7-1. Medicine dropper in plastic bottle full of water.

## *TEACHER INFORMATION*

This is called a Cartesian Diver. Fill the plastic bottle with water. Put enough water in the medicine dropper so it will just barely float in the bottle and place it in the bottle, bulb end up. Put the cap on the bottle. When pressure is exerted on the bottle, water, which will not compress, is forced into the medicine dropper to compress the air and make the dropper heavier. It will sink to the bottom of the bottle. When pressure on the bottle is released, the compressed air in the dropper will force some of the water out and the dropper will float to the surface. If pressure on the bottle is varied, the dropper can be stopped in the middle or at any point desired.

This demonstration may also be found as Activity 40 in Section 2, "Air."

# ACTIVITY 8: How Can We Watch Air Expand and Contract?

(Teacher-supervised activity)

## MATERIALS NEEDED

- Heat-resistant flask *or* a glass soda bottle
- Balloon large enough to cover bottle mouth
- Bowl of very hot (not boiling) water
- Bowl of cold water

## PROCEDURE

1. Place the mouth of a balloon over the top of the bottle. Be sure no air can escape.
2. Put the bottle in very hot (not boiling) water for a few minutes.
3. What happened?
   **CAUTION: Before moving the bottle from the hot to the cold water, wait several seconds to prevent possible cracking of the bottle.** Now place the bottle in cold water for a few minutes.
5. What happened?
6. What can you say about this?

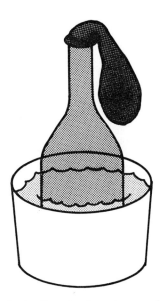

FIGURE 8-1. Bottle in bowl of water and balloon on top.

## *TEACHER INFORMATION*

When the bottle is placed in hot water, the air inside will expand and cause the balloon to inflate slightly. When the bottle is placed in cold water, the air will contract and the balloon will deflate.

This demonstration may also be found as Activity 37 in Section 2, "Air."

# ACTIVITY 9: What Is a Relationship between Moving Air and Its Pressure?

## *MATERIALS NEEDED*

- Two ping-pong balls
- Thread
- Drinking straw

## *PROCEDURE*

1. Suspend two ping-pong balls on threads, leaving approximately 2 cm. (¾ in.) between them.
2. Use a drinking straw to blow between the balls.
3. What happened? What can you say about this?

## *TEACHER INFORMATION*

When air is blown between the ping-pong balls, they will come together since the molecules of air between the balls are moving faster and create a reduced pressure.

# ACTIVITY 10: How Many Nails Can You Put Into a Full Glass of Water?

---

## *MATERIALS NEEDED*

- 8-ounce glass
- Water
- Paper and pencil

- 200 finishing nails 5 cm. (2 in.) long

## *PROCEDURE*

1. Fill an 8-ounce glass with water. Make sure the water is level with the top of the glass.
2. Get some finishing nails about 5 cm. (2 in.) long.
3. On a piece of paper, write down the number of nails you think will go into the glass before water spills over the top.
4. Carefully put the nails in one at a time, point first. What happened?
5. What can you say about this?

## *TEACHER INFORMATION*

Students will probably be able to put many nails into the glass. Smaller nails, pennies, or paper clips will also work well. Water molecules have an attraction for each other (called *cohesion*). This attraction forms a bond at the surface (called *surface tension*).Water on the surface of the glass will bulge above the rim as the molecules cling togther. Gravity soon overcomes this force, however, and the water spills over.

Water forms in drops because of surface tension.

# ACTIVITY 11: How Can Surface Tension Be Disturbed?

## *MATERIALS NEEDED*

- Saucer
- Pepper
- Liquid detergent

- Water
- Toothpicks

## *PROCEDURE*

1. Cover the bottom of the saucer with water.
2. Lightly cover the surface of the water with pepper.
3. Dip the tip of a toothpick into the center of the water. What happened?
4. Now dip the tip of another toothpick into the liquid detergent.
5. Dip the toothpick with soap on it into the middle of the saucer. What happened?
6. What can you say about this?

## *TEACHER INFORMATION*

Pepper will float on the surface of the untreated water. Because of *adhesion* (attraction of unlike molecules for each other), water molecules cling to the side of each pepper particle. The attraction of water molecules to each other at the surface (surface tension) results in a tugging effect on the pepper particle all the way around. Adding detergent breaks the surface tension on the near side and the pepper is pulled to the edge of the dish by the tugging of water molecules on the other side of the pepper particle.

## *EXTENDED ACTIVITIES*

Instead of pepper, float a staple on its side. When detergent is added, the staple will usually sink. Use the hot water. Try cold water. Try soft water. Try distilled water. What do you think will happen if you put detergent on the bulging surface of the water created in Activity 10? Try it.

# ACTIVITY 12: How Can You Make a Soap Motorboat?

## MATERIALS NEEDED

- One tongue depressor cut in half cross-wise and split down the middle
- Medicine dropper filled with liquid detergent
- Large bowl or pan of clean fresh water
- Knife (older students only)

## PROCEDURE

1. Carve one end of the tongue depressor to a point so it looks like a boat. Make a small notch in the opposite end.
2. Float your boat near the center of the pan of water.
3. Use the medicine dropper to put a small amount of detergent in the notch.. What happened?

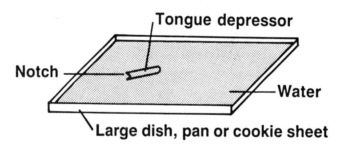

FIGURE 12-1. Tongue depressor motorboat floating in pan.

## TEACHER INFORMATION

The drop of detergent will gradually dissolve, breaking the surface tension of the water behind the boat. Water molecules tug on the boat at the front, pulling it through the water.

*Note:* If liquid detergent is not available, scrape a bit of soap from a bar of hand soap into the notched area of the boat. It will work just the same. Before attempting to repeat any activities involving soap or detergent, rinse everything thoroughly in clean water.

# ACTIVITY 13: How Do Raisins Swim?

## MATERIALS NEEDED

- Clear carbonated soda
- Pint-sized fruit jar
- 20 raisins

## PROCEDURE

1. Add clear carbonated soda to the jar until it is about two-thirds full.
2. Put about 20 raisins into the jar with the soda. Observe for several minutes. What happened? What can you say about this?

## TEACHER INFORMATION

When the raisins are put into the soda, they will sink to the bottom of the jar. Gradually, small bubbles of carbon dioxide gas from the soda will collect on the skins of the raisins. Soon, enough bubbles of gas will have collected on the surface of the raisins to make them buoyant and they will float to the surface of the soda. As soon as the raisins reach the surface, the bubbles pop and the raisins sink to the bottom. This action will continue for some time.

# ACTIVITY 14: How Can You Boil Water in a Paper Cup?

(Teacher demonstration)

## MATERIALS NEEDED

- Plastic or nonwaxed paper cup
- Candle or alcohol lamp
- Water

## PROCEDURE

1. Put about 5 cm (2 in.) of water in a plastic or paper cup.
2. Put a lit candle or alcohol lamp under the cup.
3. What happened? Can you think of a reason why?

## TEACHER INFORMATION

Soon the water will become hot enough to boil, but the paper cup will not burn. Water boils at 100° Celsius at sea level. Paper must be much hotter to reach its kindling point. As long as water remains in the cup, it will keep the paper cool enough to prevent it from burning. Remember, once water reaches its boiling point, it does not get hotter if the pressure on the surface remains the same.

# ACTIVITY 15: How Can You Make a Worm?

## *MATERIALS NEEDED*

- Soda straw with sealed paper wrapper intact
- Water
- Medicine dropper
- Small dish

## *PROCEDURE*

1. Tear the top off the paper wrapper of a soda straw so the top of the straw can be seen.
2. Put the bottom of the straw on a table and carefully slide the paper wrapper down the straw until it is wrinkled, but no more than 5 cm (2 in.) long.
3. Place the wrinkled "worm" on a small dish and use your medicine dropper to put three or four drops of water along its back.
4. What happened? What can you say about this?

FIGURE 15-1. Straw, paper wrapper, dish, and medicine dropper.

## *TEACHER INFORMATION*

When a few drops of water are put on the wrinkled paper, the "worm" will begin to grow and sometimes crawl. This is because the water spreads through the dry compressed paper and causes it to relax and expand.

Capillary action, of which this is one example, is the attraction or repulsion of liquids to solids. The study of surface tension in physics and chemistry and the science of chromatics also involve principles of capillary action. See your encyclopedia for further information. This is an excellent "take-home-and-talk-about" activity.

This demonstration is repeated as Activity 62 in Section 3, "Water."

# ACTIVITY 16: How Can You Put a Coin in a Glass Without Touching It?

## *MATERIALS NEEDED*

- Drinking glass
- Penny
- Index card cut into a square

## *PROCEDURE*

1. Put the card on the top of the glass.
2. Put the coin in the middle of the card.
3. With your middle finger, flip the card sharply so it flies off horizontally. What happened? What can you say about this?

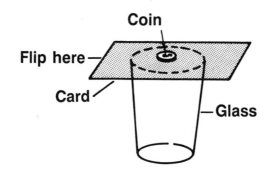

FIGURE 16-1. Glass with index card and coin.

## *TEACHER INFORMATION*

If the card is flipped horizontally with the middle finger, the coin will fall into the glass. This demonstrates the principle of inertia. The card slips from under the coin. The inertia of the coin causes it to stay in the same place, and after the card is gone the coin falls in the glass. Remember, one principle of inertia is that force is required to make a body at rest go into motion. When the card slips out, it does not apply enough force to make the coin move.

You can also pull a paper out from under a glass of water if you have the paper about half off the table and pull with a sharp downward motion. Be sure the glass is dry on the bottom.

# ACTIVITY 17: How Can You Compare Gravity and Inertia?

## *MATERIALS NEEDED*

- Two rocks of the same size
- Thin cotton thread
- Support

## *PROCEDURE*

1. Tie a thread around each rock and tie the thread to a support so the rocks hang freely.
2. Tie a second thread to each rock. These threads should hang freely from the rocks.
3. Grasp the bottom of one thread and pull down slowly.
4. What happened?
5. Now grasp the thread hanging from the second rock.
6. Pull down very sharply.
7. What happened?

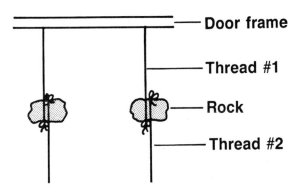

FIGURE 17-1. Two rocks hanging from threads.

## *TEACHER INFORMATION*

*Note:* The rock is suspended by one thread. Use a separate thread to hang down from the rock.

This activity demonstrates the principle of inertia. When the thread attached to the first rock is pulled slowly, the weight (pull of gravity) on the rock will help exert pressure and the thread will break above the rock. When the thread attached to the second rock is pulled sharply, the inertia of the rock (its resistance to a change in its state of motion) will overcome the pull of gravity and cause the thread to break below the rock.

To control variables, the rocks and thread should be similar, or a single rock should be used for both parts of the investigation.

# ACTIVITY 18: How Can Air Pressure Help Airplanes Fly?

## *MATERIALS NEEDED*

- One sheet of standard-sized notebook paper

## *PROCEDURE*

1. Hold the sheet of paper by the corners just below your lower lip.
2. Permit the paper to hang down in front of you.
3. Blow across the top of the paper.
4. What happened? What can you say about this?

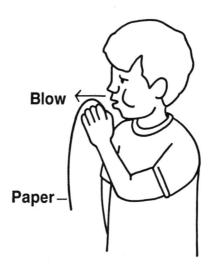

FIGURE 18-1. Student blowing air over paper.

## *TEACHER INFORMATION*

When the student blows across the top of the paper, it will rise. As air molecules move faster, their pressure is reduced and the greater air pressure below pushes the paper up. This is called *Bernoulli's principle,* and airplane wings are shaped to take advantage of this idea. The same principle is applied to draw gasoline out of the carburetor of an automobile or to draw chemicals out of the bottle of a garden-hose sprayer.

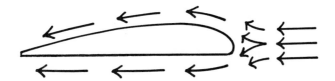

FIGURE 18-2. Air moving over and under an airplane wing.

## ADDITIONAL ACTIVITY

Place two textbooks flat on the table, leaving about 10 cm. (4 in.) of space between them. Put a sheet of notebook paper on top of the books. Blow in the space between the books. What happened to the paper? Air pressure above forces it down between the books.

# ACTIVITY 19: How Does the Moon Give Light?

## *MATERIALS NEEDED*

- Globe of earth
- White baseball-sized ball
- Flashlight

## *PROCEDURE*

1. Use a large globe of the earth.
2. Darken the room.
3. Hold the ball approximately 50 cm. (20 in.) above and behind the globe.
4. Shine a flashlight on the globe and ball.
5. Can you find reflected "moonlight" on the dark side of the globe?
6. What can you say about this?

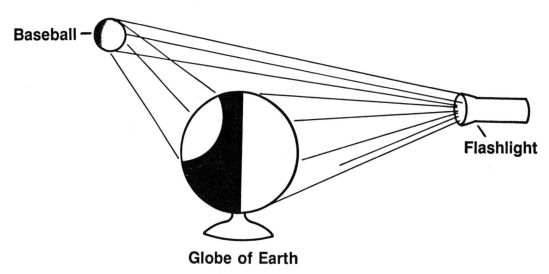

**Baseball**

**Flashlight**

**Globe of Earth**

FIGURE 19-1. Globe, ball, and flashlight.

## *TEACHER INFORMATION*

When the light is aimed toward the globe, some will strike the ball and be reflected onto the dark side. This is a way of introducing the idea of night and day and moonlight. If the white ball has about the same diameter as the width of Continental United States on the globe, they will be in approximately the correct size ratio to each other.

# ACTIVITY 20: What Is in Sea Water?

## *MATERIALS NEEDED*

- Sea water (or salt water)
- Pan

## *PROCEDURE*

1. Pour some sea water into a pan.
2. Let the water evaporate.
3. What is left in the bottom of the pan? Taste it.
4. What do you think is in sea water?

## *TEACHER INFORMATION*

Sea water contains salt, which will be left as a light-colored residue in the bottom of the pan after the water has all evaporated. For those who do not live near the ocean, a sprinkling of salt in tap water will make a good substitute.

# ACTIVITY 21: What Happens When Air Gets Warmer?

(Teacher demonstration)

## MATERIALS NEEDED

- Clear glass bowl
- 8-ounce drinking glass
- Birthday candles
- Plastic modeling clay
- Food coloring
- Rubber bands
- Matches
- Water

## PROCEDURE

1. Put about 3 cm. (1 in.) of water into the bowl. Add a drop of food coloring to the water to help you see it more clearly.
2. Put a birthday candle in the clay and stand it up in the bowl.
3. Light the candle.
4. Put the mouth of the drinking glass over the candle and into the water all the way to the bottom of the bowl.
5. What happened? What can you say about this?
6. Repeat the same activity using two, three, and four candles at a time. Use one rubber band around the glass to mark the water level each time you add a candle.
7. Can you predict what will happen if you use five candles? Try it.

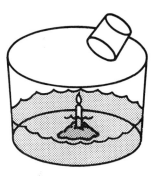

FIGURE 21-1. Bowl containing water and candles with drinking glass above.

## TEACHER INFORMATION

When the drinking glass is placed over the burning candle, the air inside will be heated and forced out. The water will prevent more air from getting in. When the candle goes out, the air inside the glass will cool and contract. Since air was forced out, there will now be less air (and air pressure) inside the glass than outside. The outside air pressure will force water up into the tumbler. Additional candles will produce more heat, causing more air to be forced out, and the water will rise higher.

This demonstration is also Activity 36 in Section 2, "Air."

## ENRICHMENT ACTIVITY

How is this related to Activity 1, "What Can Air Do to an Egg?" in this section?

# ACTIVITY 22: How Does Air Pressure Affect Water Flow?

(Do this over a sink or bucket)

## MATERIALS NEEDED

- Gallon or quart metal can with tight-fitting lid and a hole punched into the side near the bottom
- Masking tape
- Water
- Sink or bucket

## PROCEDURE

1. There is a small hole near the bottom of the can. Find it and cover it with a piece of masking tape.
2. Fill the can with water.
3. Remove the masking tape and observe the stream of water.
4. Put the lid on the can tightly. Observe the stream of water. What happened?
5. Listen carefully as you loosen the lid. What happened?
6. What can you say about this?

## TEACHER INFORMATION

Be sure the lid seals so the container is airtight. Without the lid, water will flow in a stream from the hole. When the lid is on tight, the water flow will gradually stop even though water still remains in the can. When the lid is removed, you will probably hear a hissing and perhaps a metallic sound. A metallic sound indicates the sides of the can are being pushed back into place. The water will flow from the hole again.

Without a lid, air exerts pressure on the top of the water in the can. With the lid in place, air can no longer enter the can. As the volume of water decreases, air inside the can will replace it but its pressure will be reduced. It "thins out" to occupy more space. Air pressure outside the can remains the same. When the outside air pressure becomes greater than the air pressure inside the can, the flow of water will stop.

*Note:* A rigid plastic bottle can be used in place of the metal can.

## ENRICHMENT QUESTIONS

1. Why is the hole in a pop-top can shaped the way it is?
2. Why do you punch two holes in the solid lid of a juice can?
3. There are usually open plumbing pipes sticking out of the roof of your house or apartment. Why?

# ACTIVITY 23: What Is Water Pressure?

(Teacher-supervised partners; do this over a sink or bucket)

## MATERIALS NEEDED

- Metal cans of different shapes and sizes
- Cardboard and plastic containers of various sizes and shapes (milk carton, frozen juice cans, foam cups, etc.)

- Masking tape
- Nail or sharp puncher
- Hammer
- Water
- Sink or large bucket

## PROCEDURE

1. Use a nail to punch a hole into the side very near the bottom of each container.
2. Cover each hole with masking tape.
3. Choose two containers of different size but the same shape.
4. Add water to the same depth in both containers. Do not put a lid or top on.
5. Be sure the taped holes are at the edge of the sink or bucket.
6. Carefully remove the tapes at the same time. Compare the stream of water from each container.
7. Repeat the activity using different-sized and different-shaped containers. Be sure always to fill them to the same depth.
8. What can you say about this?

## TEACHER INFORMATION

If possible, punch holes in the containers in advance. Regardless of the size or shape of the container, the stream of water at any depth will be the same. Water pressure, which can be measured by the distance of the stream of water as it is forced out of the hole, depends only on the depth or height of the column of water.

Be sure the holes in the containers are the same size. Always fill the containers to the same depth. With large containers, the stream of water will continue for a longer time but will not go a greater distance. Knowing the depth of the water, not the volume of the water, is important to the safety of divers.

# Section 2

## AIR

# TO THE TEACHER

A fundamental understanding of air is important to further studies in such areas as weather, air flight, plants and animals, and pollution. Although children live in an ocean of air, they often have difficulty realizing it really exists.

The following activities have been developed and used with middle graders. Most can be adapted for use with younger and older students. Activities 34 through 43 are especially important as background information for a study of weather.

# ACTIVITY 24: How Can You Test to See If Air Is in Something?

## *MATERIALS NEEDED*

- 8-ounce clear plastic tumbler
- Facial tissue
- Deep bowl filled with water

## *PROCEDURE*

1. Look at the glass. What is in it?
2. Crumple the tissue and put it in the bottom of the glass.
3. Turn the glass over (be sure the tissue does not fall out) and push it, mouth first, into a deep bowl of water.
4. Now remove the glass without tipping it.
5. What happened to the tissue?
6. What can you say about this?

FIGURE 24-1. Bowl of water with inverted cup at bottom.

## *TEACHER INFORMATION*

When the glass is lowered mouth first into the bowl of water, the air will be trapped inside and prevent water from entering the glass. Thus, the tissue will remain dry.

# ACTIVITY 25: How Can You See Air Move?

## *MATERIALS NEEDED*

- Two 8-ounce plastic tumblers marked A and B
- Deep bowl filled with water

## *PROCEDURE*

1. Look at the glasses marked A and B. What is in them?
2. Push glass A, mouth first, into the bowl of water.
3. Turn it on its side. What happened?
4. Push glass B to the bottom of the bowl, mouth first.
5. Put the mouth of glass A right above glass B and slowly tip glass B on its side.
6. What happened? What can you say about this?

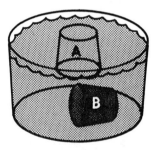

FIGURE 25-1. Bowl of water containing glass A above glass B.

## *TEACHER INFORMATION*

When glass A is pushed into the bowl, it will contain air. When it is tipped on its side, the air will bubble out and the glass will fill with water. When glass B is pushed to the bottom and tipped on its side, and if the mouth of glass A is directly above it, the air will bubble from glass B into glass A because air is lighter than water. Students will be able to see the air travel from glass B and force the water from glass A.

# ACTIVITY 26: How Can You Tell If Air Has Weight?

## *MATERIALS NEEDED*

- Meter stick
- String
- Pencil eraser
- Balloon

## *PROCEDURE*

1. Use string to suspend a meter stick in the middle. In one end of a 15-cm. (6-in.) length of string, make a loop to fit over the end of the meter stick. Tie a pencil eraser to the other end of the string.
2. Tie another loop in a 15-cm. (6-in.) string and tie an empty balloon on the other end with a bow knot. Suspend the balloon 3 cm. (1 in.) in from the end of the meter stick and balance it by moving the eraser on the other end of the meter stick. Mark where the eraser loop is on the meter stick.
3. Remove the balloon and inflate it. Retie the balloon in the same place (3 cm., or 1 in., from the end). Does it balance? What can you say about this?

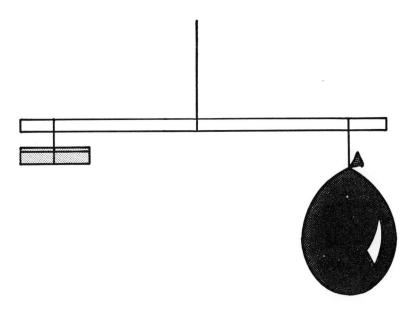

FIGURE 26-1. Eraser on balance with balloon.

## *TEACHER INFORMATION*

When the balloon is inflated and rehung on the meter stick, it will tip the balance down, showing that air has weight. Make certain the eraser does not move while the balloon is being removed and inflated.

# ACTIVITY 27: How Can You Feel the Weight and Pressure of Air?

## *MATERIALS NEEDED*

- Large, wide-mouthed, clear glass jar
- Circle of heavy, clear plastic with a diameter of at least 45 cm. (18 in.)
- String

## *PROCEDURE*

1. Push the plastic sheet down inside the bottle with about 5 cm. (2 in.) hanging over the rim.
2. Wrap the string twice around the rim of the bottle, just below the threads, and tie it tightly (the plastic should be under the string all the way around).
3. Reach inside the jar and pull the plastic upward.
4. What happened? What can you say about this?

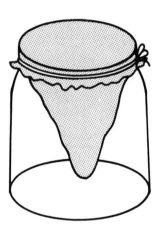

FIGURE 27-1. Plastic hanging inside glass jar.

## *TEACHER INFORMATION*

When the student pulls up on the plastic, the space inside the bottle is increased and the air pressure is reduced. The outside air pushing down on the plastic will keep it from being pulled out. You can feel the weight of the air. This can be a group activity, but be sure each child has a chance to feel the pressure.

# ACTIVITY 28: In Which Directions Will Air Pressure Push? (Part One)

___

(Teacher-supervised activity)

## *MATERIALS NEEDED*

- Clean duplicating fluid can
- Hot plate
- One cup of water

## *PROCEDURE*

1. Put about one cup of water in a clean ditto fluid can.
2. Boil the water *with the lid off.*
3. Remove the can from the stove and put the lid on tightly.
4. Observe what happens to the can.

## *TEACHER INFORMATION*

When heated, the water changes to steam and drives most of the air from the can. When the lid is put on tightly, no air can get back in. As the steam inside the can cools, it condenses and returns to a liquid, and a vacuum is created. The air pressure outside the can will become much greater than the air inside and will gradually crush the can.

# ACTIVITY 29: In Which Directions Will Air Pressure Push? (Part Two)

(Do this over the sink, please)

## MATERIALS NEEDED

- 8-ounce glass
- 5" × 8" index card
- Water

## PROCEDURE

1. Fill the glass with water (not too full).
2. Put the index card over the mouth of the glass.
3. Gently hold the card in one hand, the glass in the other.
4. Turn the glass upside down and carefully remove your hand from the card.
5. Slowly turn the glass right side up, but don't touch the card.
6. What happened?
7. What can you say about this?

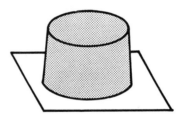

FIGURE 29-1. Inverted glass of water over card.

## TEACHER INFORMATION

When the glass full of water is turned upside down and the hand removed, the card will stay on the glass and the water will not come out. This is because the pressure of the air pushing on the card is great enough to hold the water in. When the glass is turned right side up, the card will stay on the glass, showing that air pushes in all directions.

# ACTIVITY 30: What Is Another Way to Feel Air Pressure?

---

## MATERIALS NEEDED

- Two suction-cup plungers
- Water

## PROCEDURE

1. Moisten the edges of the two plungers. Find a friend.
2. Push the ends of both plungers together. Now pull them apart.
3. What happened?
4. What can you say about this?

## TEACHER INFORMATION

When the plungers are pushed together, much of the air between them is forced out, creating a partial vacuum. The outside air pressure keeps them together. Plungers will not work on the moon because there is practically no air pressure.

# ACTIVITY 31: How Can Air Pressure Make Things Stronger?

---

## *MATERIALS NEEDED*

- Paper straws
- Potato

## *PROCEDURE*

1. Hold a straw near one end and try to stick the other end in a potato. What happened?
2. Place your finger over the top of the straw and stick the other end into the potato (do it fast and hard). What happened?
3. What can you say about this?

## *TEACHER INFORMATION*

When you try to stick the straw with both ends open in the potato, the straw will bend. When you place your finger over the upper end of the straw, the air is trapped inside and the column is strengthened. The straw will go into the potato. (Be sure to stab rapidly and hold the straw near the top during all parts of the activity.)

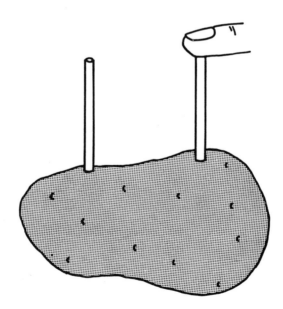

FIGURE 31-1. Potato with straws inserted.

# ACTIVITY 32: How Hard Can Air Push?

## *MATERIALS NEEDED*

- Clear glass soda bottle
- Large, long balloon

## *PROCEDURE*

1. Put the balloon into the soda bottle. Hold onto the balloon's open end.
2. Stretch the lip of the balloon over the mouth of the bottle.
3. Inflate the balloon inside the bottle.
4. What happened? Can you explain why?

FIGURE 32-1. Soda bottle with balloon hanging inside.

## *TEACHER INFORMATION*

When the child blows into the balloon, the increased air pressure inside the balloon will push against the air trapped in the bottle. The pressure of the air in the bottle will increase and push harder on the balloon. The child will discover the balloon cannot be inflated inside the bottle. Remember, the lip of the balloon must cover the mouth of the bottle to completely seal it.

# ACTIVITY 33:  How Can Air Help Us Drink?

## *MATERIALS NEEDED*

- Clear glass soda bottle filled with water
- Plastic or paper straw
- Modeling clay

## *PROCEDURE*

1.  Drink some water through the straw.
2.  Use clay to seal the top of the bottle all around the straw.
3.  Drink some more water through the straw.
4.  What happened? What can you say about this?

## *TEACHER INFORMATION*

In order to drink through a straw, you must have air pushing on the surface of the water. When the top of the bottle is sealed, air cannot get in to push, so drinking is impossible. Soda cans have either two holes or one hole shaped in such a way that air can get in as the liquid pours out; narrow-necked bottles "gurgle" because they don't.

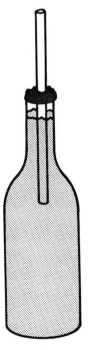

FIGURE 33-1. Soda bottle with straw sealed to the top.

# ACTIVITY 34: How Can You Tell That Warm Air Rises?

(Teacher demonstration or supervised activity)

## *MATERIALS NEEDED*

- Hot plate
- Compass
- Paper

- Thread
- Scissors

## *PROCEDURE*

1. With a compass, draw a circle with a 20-cm. (8-in.) radius. Cut out the circle with scissors. Cut a spiral about 1 cm. thick by starting on the outside of the circle and moving in to the center as you cut. Suspend your spiral by a thread attached in the center.
2. Hold the spiral over your head and blow gently. Did your spiral turn? Hold your spiral over a hot plate which has been turned on low heat. Do not let your spiral touch the hot plate.
3. What does this tell you about warm air?

## *TEACHER INFORMATION*

When you blow on the spiral it will turn. When you hold the spiral over the hot plate it will turn in the same manner. This shows that the heated air above the hot plate is rising or blowing upward just as you were.

# ACTIVITY 35: What Happens When Air Is Heated?

(Teacher demonstration)

## MATERIALS NEEDED

- Masking tape
- Meter stick
- Lit candle
- Chair
- Two lunch-sized paper bags

## PROCEDURE

1. Use masking tape to attach a lunch-sized paper bag, open end down, to each end of the meter stick.
2. Balance the meter stick on the back of a chair.
3. Carefully put a lit candle under the open end of one of the paper bags.
4. What happened?
5. What can you say about this?

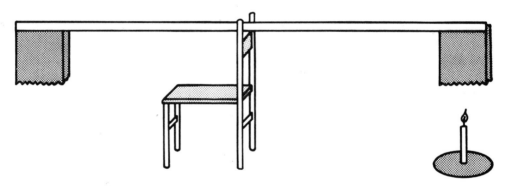

FIGURE 35-1. Paper bags balanced on chair.

## TEACHER INFORMATION

**CAUTION: Do this activity over a hard, nonflammable surface.**

As the air in the paper bag above the candle is heated, the rapid movement of molecules causes the air to expand, and as some of the air inside is forced out, the air in the bag becomes lighter. The paper bag will begin to rise. This is the same principle hot-air balloons use.

## ENRICHMENT ACTIVITY

Hot-air ballooning has become very popular recently. Flying safely requires a great deal of skill and knowledge, so balloon pilots must be licensed. Find out all you can about hot-air ballooning. Can it be done near your home?

# ACTIVITY 36: What Happens When Air Gets Warmer?

(Teacher demonstration)

## MATERIALS NEEDED

- Clear glass bowl
- 8-ounce drinking glass
- Birthday candles
- Plastic modeling clay
- Food coloring
- Rubber bands
- Matches
- Water

## PROCEDURE

1. Put about 3 cm. (1 in.) of water into the bowl. Add a drop of food coloring to the water to help you see it more clearly.
2. Put a birthday candle in the clay and stand it up in the bowl.
3. Light the candle.
4. Put the mouth of the drinking glass over the candle and into the water all the way to the bottom of the bowl.
5. What happened? What can you say about this?
6. Repeat the same activity using two, three, and four candles at a time. Use one rubber band around the glass to mark the water level each time you add a candle.
7. Can you predict what will happen if you use five candles? Try it.

FIGURE 36-1. Bowl containing water and candles with drinking glass above.

## TEACHER INFORMATION

When the drinking glass is placed over the burning candle, the air inside will be heated and forced out. The water will prevent more air from getting in. When the candle goes out, the air inside the glass will cool and contract. Since air was forced out, there will now be less air (and air pressure) inside the glass than outside. The outside air pressure will force water up into the tumbler. Additional candles will produce more heat, causing more air to be forced out, and the water will rise higher.

## ENRICHMENT ACTIVITY

How is this related to Activity 1, "What Can Air Do to an Egg?" in Section 1?

# ACTIVITY 37: How Can We Watch Air Expand and Contract?

(Teacher-supervised activity)

## *MATERIALS NEEDED*

- Heat-resistant flask *or* a glass soda bottle
- Balloon large enough to cover bottle mouth
- Bowl of very hot (not boiling) water
- Bowl of cold water

## *PROCEDURE*

1. Place the mouth of a balloon over the top of the bottle. Be sure no air can escape.
2. Put the bottle in very hot (not boiling) water for a few minutes.
3. What happened?
4. **CAUTION: Before moving the bottle from the hot to the cold water, wait several seconds to prevent possible cracking of the bottle.** Now place the bottle in cold water for a few minutes.
5. What happened?
6. What can you say about this?

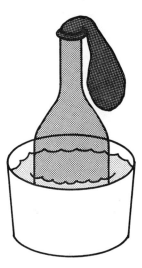

FIGURE 37-1. Bottle in bowl of water and balloon on top.

## *TEACHER INFORMATION*

When the bottle is placed in hot water, the air inside will expand and cause the balloon to inflate slightly. When the bottle is placed in cold water, the air will contract and the balloon will deflate.

# ACTIVITY 38: How Does Cold Air Behave?

(Teacher demonstration)

## MATERIALS NEEDED

- Hemp rope or incense
- Flashlight
- Refrigerator
- Match

## PROCEDURE

1. Light a hemp rope or use incense to make smoke. Observe how the smoke behaves.
2. Put the smoking object in the freezer compartment of a refrigerator.
3. Close the refrigerator door and darken the room.
4. Open the freezer compartment door and use a flashlight to observe the smoke.
5. What happened? What can you say about this?

## TEACHER INFORMATION

In air at room temperature the smoke will rise. When it mixes with cold air in the freezer compartment, it will sink with the cold air when the door is opened. Cold air contains more molecules per cubic centimeter and therefore is heavier.

*Note:* Be sure to blow all the smoky air out of the refrigerator at the conclusion of the demonstration.

# ACTIVITY 39: What Happens When Warm Air and Cold Air Mix?

## *MATERIALS NEEDED*

- Two quart-sized glass jars
- Pan of hot water
- Hemp rope or incense
- Ice cubes
- Flashlight
- Match

## *PROCEDURE*

1. Put one jar upright in the pan of hot water.
2. Have your teacher put smoke in the two jars.
3. Then stand the second jar upside down on the first bottle with the mouths together.
4. Put several ice cubes on top of the upper jar.
5. Darken the room. Use a flashlight to observe the smoke.
6. What happened? What can you say about this?

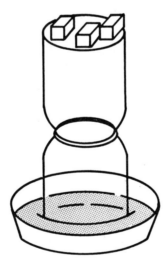

FIGURE 39-1. Jar inverted on another, which is standing in a pan of water.

## *TEACHER INFORMATION*

The air in the bottom jar will be heated and rise. When it nears the top of the second bottle, it will cool and begin to sink. Air currents will swirl in the two jars.

When you open a window too cool off a room, another window should be opened above or below the first, if possible, so the air can circulate.

# ACTIVITY 40: How Can Air Be Compressed?

## *MATERIALS NEEDED*

- Clear plastic 16-ounce shampoo bottle filled with water
- Medicine dropper filled with a small amount of water

## *PROCEDURE*

1. Observe the medicine dropper in the bottle.
2. Gently squeeze the bottle.
3. What happened? What can you say about this?

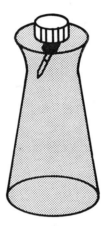

FIGURE 40-1. Medicine dropper in plastic bottle full of water.

## *TEACHER INFORMATION*

This is called a Cartesian Diver. Fill the plastic bottle with water. Put enough water in the medicine dropper so it will just barely float in the bottle and place the dropper in the bottle, bulb end up. Put the cap on the bottle. When pressure is exerted on the bottle, water, which will not compress, is forced into the medicine dropper to compress the air and make the dropper heavier. It will sink to the bottom of the bottle. When pressure on the bottle is released, the compressed air in the dropper will force some of the water out and the dropper will float to the surface. If pressure on the bottle is varied, the dropper can be stopped in the middle or at any point desired.

# ACTIVITY 41: What Is Another Way Air Can Be Compressed?

## *MATERIALS NEEDED*

- 12- or 16-ounce clear soda bottle
- Head from wooden kitchen match
- Water

## *PROCEDURE*

1. Float a head from a kitchen match in a soda bottle completely full of water.
2. Use your thumb to push down on the water in the mouth of the bottle. Your thumb should completely cover the bottle's mouth.
3. What happened? What can you say about this?

FIGURE 41-1. Match head in soda bottle full of water.

## *TEACHER INFORMATION*

This is another Cartesian Diver. The match head is porous—full of air spaces—so it floats on top of the water. When you use your thumb to push on the surface, water is forced into the air spaces in the match head and it will sink. When the pressure is released, the match head will float to the surface again as the compressed air in the match head forces the water out.

*Note:* The thumb must cover the mouth of the bottle completely. For young children, you may need to find a bottle with a narrower mouth.

# ACTIVITY 42: How Can You Get Water Out of the Air?

---

## *MATERIALS NEEDED*

- Ice cubes
- Clear 8-ounce glass tumbler
- Sheet of white paper
- Food coloring
- Water

## *PROCEDURE*

1. Put several ice cubes in the tumbler. Fill the glass with water.
2. Add a drop of food coloring to the water and stir.
3. Put the tumbler on a piece of white paper and let it stand for several minutes.
4. What happened? What can you say about this?

## *TEACHER INFORMATION*

When air is cooled it gives up moisture. As the tumbler becomes cold, the air around it will be cooled and moisture will condense on it. Food coloring and the white paper are used to show that the water is not passing through the tumbler. The water formed on the outside will be clear. We often use coasters under cold drink glasses because of condensation.

# ACTIVITY 43: How Can You Make Rain?

(Teacher-supervised activity)

## *MATERIALS NEEDED*

- Quart-sized glass jar
- Aluminum or iron pie tin
- Hot water
- Ice cubes

## *PROCEDURE*

1. Pour a cup of hot water in a quart-sized glass jar. (No lid is needed.)
2. Put some ice cubes in a pie tin and place it on top of the jar.
3. Observe for several minutes. What happened?

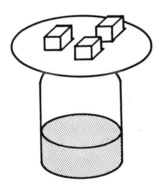

FIGURE 43-1. Jar with water in bottom and ice cubes on top.

## *TEACHER INFORMATION*

The hot water will heat the air in the jar and add moisture to it. The moisture-laden hot air will rise. As it nears the cold pie tin, the air will cool and condense. In time, it may actually begin to rain outside the jar, as water drops form on, and fall from, the part of the pan overhanging the jar. (This demonstration is repeated in Section 3, "Water, Activity 46.)

## *ENRICHMENT ACTIVITY*

If you added some smoke to the air inside the bottle, what would you see?

# Section 3

---

# WATER

# TO THE TEACHER

---

Water is essential to all forms of life. People can live for weeks without food but only for a short period of time without water. Because it is usually available we often take it for granted, yet it plays an important role in almost every area of science. Even the study of nonliving materials includes the study of how water acts upon and interacts with them

Many of the activities in this section appear in other parts of the book. In combination with several new activities, they provide a basis for an independent study of water, apart from its relationships to other areas of science.

# ACTIVITY 44: How Does Water Disappear?

## *MATERIALS NEEDED*

- Sponge
- Chalkboard
- Water
- Heavy piece of cardboard

## *PROCEDURE*

1. Moisten the sponge.
2. Make a wide, damp streak on the blackboard.
3. Observe for several minutes. What happened?
4. Make two streaks about 1 m. (1 yd.) apart.
5. Use the cardboard to fan one of the streaks.
6. Compare the time it took for each to disappear.

## *TEACHER INFORMATION*

This is an initial experience with evaporation. If the sponge is just moist the results will be faster than if it is soaking wet.

Using the cardboard as a fan will increase the rate of evaporation.

An alternate activity is to put a small amount of water—1 cm. (½ in.)—in two small jars. Seal the lid of one and leave the other open. Observe for 24 hours.

Students should learn from this activity that water is absorbed into the air by a process called evaporation. Increasing the amount of air moving over the water (fanning) increases the rate of evaporation. The amount of moisture the air already contains (humidity) will be a factor. (See Section 4, "Weather.")

# ACTIVITY 45: What Is Condensation?

---

(Teacher-supervised activity)

## *MATERIALS NEEDED*

- Metal pan (or beaker)
- Water
- Heat source

- Sheet of glass or hand mirror (preferably cold)

## *PROCEDURE*

1. Put about 1 cm. (½ in.) of water in the pan.
2. Heat the water until it boils.
3. Hold the sheet of glass over the boiling water.
4. Observe the glass carefully. What do you see forming on the bottom of the glass? Explain why you think this happens.

## *TEACHER INFORMATION*

As water is heated, the rate of evaporation is increased. The sheet of glass or mirror held over the escaping water vapor cools the vapor and causes it to condense into liquid form, shown by the drops of water forming on the bottom. This process will be speeded up if the mirror or sheet of glass is cooled first, but this can be dangerous because of the risk of breaking the glass.

Similar evidence of condensation can be observed by placing a pitcher (or other container) of ice water out on a table. Water vapor in the air is cooled by the pitcher and drops of water form on its surface.

# ACTIVITY 46: How Can You Make Rain?

(Teacher-supervised activity)

## MATERIALS NEEDED

- Quart-sized glass jar
- Aluminum or iron pie tin
- Hot water
- Ice cubes

## PROCEDURE

1. Pour a cup of hot water in a quart-sized glass jar. (No lid is needed.)
2. Put some ice cubes in a pie tin and place it on top of the jar.
3. Observe for several minutes. What happened?

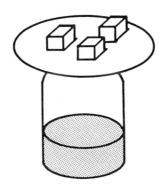

FIGURE 46-1. Jar with water in bottom and ice cubes on top.

## TEACHER INFORMATION

The hot water will heat the air in the jar and add moisture to it. The moisture-laden hot air will rise. As it nears the cold pie tin, the air will cool and condense. In time, it may actually begin to "rain" outside the jar, as water drops form on, and fall from, the part of the pan overhanging the jar.

## ENRICHMENT ACTIVITY

If you added some smoke to the air inside the bottle, what would you see?

# ACTIVITY 47: How Can You Get Water Out of the Air?

## MATERIALS NEEDED

- Ice cubes
- Clear 8-ounce glass tumbler
- Sheet of white paper
- Food coloring
- Water

## PROCEDURE

1. Put several ice cubes in the tumbler. Fill the glass with water.
2. Add a drop of food coloring to the water and stir.
3. Put the tumbler on a piece of white paper and let it stand for several minutes.
4. What happened? What can you say about this?

## TEACHER INFORMATION

When air is cooled it gives up moisture. As the tumbler becomes cold, the air around it will be cooled and moisture will condense on it. Food coloring and the white paper are used to show that the water is not passing through the tumbler. The water formed on the outside will be clear. We often use coasters under cold drink glasses because of condensation. (See Section 2, Activity 42.)

# ACTIVITY 48: What Is Another Way to Get Moisture Out of the Air?

(Teacher demonstration)

## *MATERIALS NEEDED*

- Large, wide-mouthed clear glass jar
- String
- Kitchen matches
- Circle of heavy clear plastic with a diameter of at least 45 cm. (18 in.)
- Water

## *PROCEDURE*

1. Pour a cup of water into the jar.
2. Light a kitchen match. Hold it down in the jar to make smoke.
3. Quickly push the plastic sheet down inside the jar with about 5 cm. (2 in.) hanging over the rim. (Don't let the smoke escape.)
4. Wrap the string twice around the rim of the jar just below the threads and tie it tightly. (The plastic should be under the string.)
5. Reach inside and pull up sharply on the plastic.
6. What happened? What can you say about this?

FIGURE 48-1. Plastic hanging inside glass jar.

## *TEACHER INFORMATION*

These are the same basic materials used in Activity 27. Adding water to the jar provides additional moisture, and smoke provides tiny particles in the air. When you pull up sharply on the plastic, air pressure in the jar is reduced and the air suddenly becomes cooler. Cool air cannot hold as much moisture as warm air, so tiny droplets of water form around the smoke particles and make a cloud. The cloud will form for only an instant before disappearing, but you can usually make it form several times.

# ACTIVITY 49: How Can You Boil Water in a Paper Cup?

(Teacher demonstration)

## MATERIALS NEEDED

- Plastic or nonwaxed paper cup
- Candle or alcohol lamp
- Water

## PROCEDURE

1. Put about 5 cm. (2 in.) of water in a plastic or paper cup.
2. Put a candle or alcohol lamp under the cup.
3. What happened? Can you think of a reason why?

## TEACHER INFORMATION

Soon the water will become hot enough to boil, but the paper cup will not burn. Water boils at 100° Celsius at sea level. Paper must be much hotter to reach its kindling point. As long as water remains in the cup, it will keep the paper cool enough to prevent it from burning. Remember, once water reaches its boiling point, it does not get hotter if the pressure on the surface remains the same.

If the pressure on the surface of the water is increased, the boiling point will be increased and the water can become hotter (as in a pressure cooker). If the pressure on the surface is decreased, water will boil at a lower temperature, which is why high-altitude cooking requires more time.

# ACTIVITY 50: How Can We See Water Pressure?

## *MATERIALS NEEDED*

- Gallon can or plastic bottle
- Nail
- Hammer

## *PROCEDURE*

1. Use the nail to punch three holes, equally spaced from top to bottom, in the can or plastic bottle.
2. Place the container in the sink and hold all three holes while filling it with water.
3. Release all three holes at the same time.
4. What happened? What does this tell you about the weight and pressure of water?

## *TEACHER INFORMATION*

The stream of water will be greatest from the lowest hole. Less will flow from the middle hole and least from the top hole.

This demonstrates that the pressure of water increases with its depth. (This is also true of air pressure. Pressure at sea level is much greater than at 10,000 feet.)

# ACTIVITY 51: How Many Nails Can You Put into a Full Glass of Water?

___

## *MATERIALS NEEDED*

- 8-ounce glass
- Water
- Paper and pencil

- 200 finishing nails 5 cm. (2 in.) long

## *PROCEDURE*

1. Fill an 8-ounce glass with water. Make sure the water is level with the top of the glass.
2. Get some finishing nails about 5 cm. (2 in.) long.
3. On a piece of paper, write down the number of nails you think will go into the glass before water spills over the top.
4. Carefully put the nails in one at a time, point first. What happened?
5. What can you say about this?

## *TEACHER INFORMATION*

Students will probably be able to put many nails into the glass. Smaller nails, pennies, or paper clips will also work well. Water molecules have an attraction for each other (called *cohesion*). This attraction forms a bond at the surface (called *surface tension*). Water on the surface of the glass will bulge above the rim as the molecules cling together. Gravity soon overcomes this force, however, and the water spills over.

Water forms in drops because of surface tension.

# ACTIVITY 52: How Can Surface Tension Be Disturbed?

## MATERIALS NEEDED

- Saucer
- Pepper
- Liquid detergent
- Water
- Toothpicks

## PROCEDURE

1. Cover the bottom of the saucer with water.
2. Lightly cover the surface of the water with pepper.
3. Dip the tip of a toothpick into the center of the water. What happened?
4. Now dip the tip of another toothpick into the liquid detergent.
5. Dip the toothpick with soap on it into the middle of the saucer. What happened?
6. What can you say about this?

## TEACHER INFORMATION

Pepper will float on the surface of the untreated water. Because of *adhesion* (attraction of unlike molecules for each other), water molecules cling to the side of each pepper particle. The attraction of water molecules to each other at the surface *(surface tension)* results in a tugging effect on the pepper particle all the way around. Adding detergent breaks the surface tension on the near side and the pepper is pulled to the edge of the dish by the tugging of water molecules on the other side of the pepper particle.

## EXTENDED ACTIVITY

Instead of pepper, float a staple on its side. When detergent is added, the staple will usually sink. Use hot water. Try cold water. Try soft water. Try distilled water. What do you think will happen if you put detergent on the bulging surface of the water created in Activity 51? Try it.

# ACTIVITY 53: How Can You Make a Soap Motorboat?

## *MATERIALS NEEDED*

- One tongue depressor cut in half cross-wise and split down the middle
- Medicine dropper filled with liquid detergent

- Large bowl or pan of clean fresh water
- Knife (older students only)

## *PROCEDURE*

1. Carve one end of the tongue depressor to a point so it looks like a boat. Make a small notch in the opposite end.
2. Float your boat near the center of the pan of water.
3. Use the medicine dropper to put a small amount of detergent in the notch. What happened?

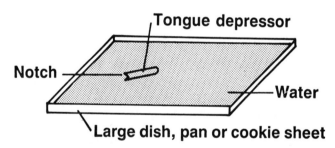

FIGURE 53-1. Tongue depressor motorboat floating in pan.

## *TEACHER INFORMATION*

The drop of detergent will gradually dissolve, breaking the surface tension of the water behind the boat. Water molecules tug on the boat at the front, pulling it through the water.

*Note:* If liquid detergent is not available, scrape a bit of soap from a bar of hand soap into the notched area of the boat. It will work just the same. Before attempting to repeat any activities involving soap or detergent, rinse everything thoroughly in clean water.

# ACTIVITY 54: How Can You Pour Light?

(Enrichment activity)

## *MATERIALS NEEDED*

- Tall slim jar (olive jar)
- Flashlight
- Hammer
- Nail
- Newspaper or light cardboard
- Masking tape or plastic tape
- Water

## *PROCEDURE*

1. With the hammer and nail, make two holes in the lid of the jar. The holes should be near the edge but opposite each other. One hole should be quite small. Work the nail around in the other to enlarge the hole a bit.
2. Fill the jar about two-thirds full of water and put the lid on.
3. Put tape over the holes in the lid until you are ready to pour.
4. Lay the jar and flashlight end to end, with the face of the flashlight at the bottom of the jar.
5. Roll the newspaper or cardboard around the jar and flashlight to enclose them in a light-tight tube. Tape the tube together so it will stay.
6. Slide the flashlight out of the tube, turn it on, and slide it back into the tube.
7. Hold the apparatus upright and remove the tape from the lid. With the large nail hole down, pour the water into the pan.
8. What happened to the beam of light as the water poured into the pan?
9. Do you have any idea what causes this?

## *TEACHER INFORMATION*

Although light travels in straight lines, it is reflected internally at the water's surface and follows the path of the stream of water. Because of the phenomenon of internal reflection, fiber optics can be used to direct light anywhere a wire can go, even into the veins and arteries of the human body.

Generally refraction occurs as light changes speed passing from one medium to another such as in Activity 57.

Reflection commonly refers to the reproduction of an image or light in a single medium, in this case water or plastic.

# ACTIVITY 55: How Can a Water Drop Make Things Larger?

## MATERIALS NEEDED

- Thin copper wire 6–8 in. long
- Nail 8 cm. (3 in.) long
- Water
- Book

## PROCEDURE

1. Make a small loop in the end of the wire. You may want to wrap it around the nail to make it the correct size.
2. Capture a drop of water in the loop.
3. Use the drop of water in the loop to look at print in a book. What happened? What can you say about this?
4. Gently tap the wire. Try to get most of the water drop out of the loop (a little must remain all across it).
5. Look at the print again. What happened? What can you say about this?

## TEACHER INFORMATION

This activity can be used to introduce the concept of light being bent as it travels through different media. The water drop acts as a convex lens and makes objects appear larger. The thin film in the loop works as a concave lens and make things appear smaller.

For younger children, you may want to put a drop of water on printed paper. The print will be magnified.

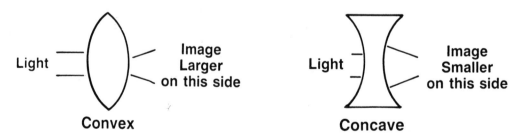

FIGURE 55-1. Convex and concave lenses.

# ACTIVITY 56: How Can Water Make a Coin Appear?

## *MATERIALS NEEDED*

- Opaque bowl
- Coin
- Water

## *PROCEDURE*

1. Put the coin in the bowl. Mark the spot so you're sure it doesn't move.
2. Put the bowl on the table and crouch down until you can no longer see the coin. (Don't go down too far—just until you can no longer see the coin.)
3. Have a friend slowly pour water into the bowl. What happened?
4. What can you say about this?

## *TEACHER INFORMATION*

Light travels in what appears to be a straight line in air, but when it goes through water, it slows down and is bent. As water is poured into the bowl, the light will bend and more of the bottom of the bowl will be exposed. The coin will appear.

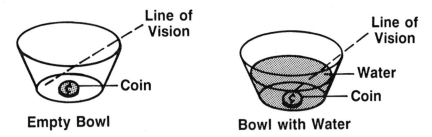

FIGURE 56-1. Diagrams of bowl and coin showing how water bends light.

# ACTIVITY 57: What Do Bears Know That Many People Don't?

## *MATERIALS NEEDED*

- 8-ounce water glass
- Pencil
- Water

## *PROCEDURE*

1. Use an 8-ounce glass about two-thirds full of water.
2. Put a pencil in the glass. Observe the pencil at above and below the water level.
3. What can you say about this?
4. Why do you think this might be called "What do bears know that people don't?" Think of a bear trying to catch a fish it sees in the water.

## *TEACHER INFORMATION*

When the pencil is put in the glass of water, it appears to bend as it enters the water. This is because the light is bent as it travels through the water. Actually, the pencil is not where it appears to be under the water. Bears seem to know this and use it when fishing. They know where the fish is even though it isn't exactly where it appears to be.

Children may also notice that the pencil appears bigger under the water. This is because the curved surface of the glass and the water in it act like a convex lens.

# ACTIVITY 58: What Can You Learn From an Egg?

## *MATERIALS NEEDED*

- Raw egg
- Hard-boiled egg
- Glass full of water
- Salt

## *PROCEDURE*

1. One of these eggs is raw and the other hard-boiled. Can you tell which is which?
2. Peel the hard-boiled egg.
3. Put it in a glass of water.
4. Add salt, a tablespoon at a time, until something happens to the egg. What happened?
5. What can you say about this?

## *TEACHER INFORMATION*

When the peeled egg is put in the untreated water, it will sink to the bottom of the glass. As salt is added to the water, the egg will rise and float on top. This is because salt increases the density of the water until the egg is able to float.

Floating an egg in brine solution is the method some people use to tell when the brine is just right for pickling.

# ACTIVITY 59:  How Does a Hydrometer Work?

## *MATERIALS NEEDED*

- Lipstick tube cap
- Several small nails (or screws)
- Tape (or gummed label)
- Marker

- Plastic tumbler
- Water
- Salt
- A variety of liquids
- Paper and pencil

## *PROCEDURE*

1. Fill the tumbler about two-thirds full of water.
2. Place 8 or 10 weights (small nails or screws) in the lipstick cap.
3. Put the gummed label or a piece of tape lengthwise on the lipstick cap.
4. Place the lipstick cap, open end up, in the glass of water. Add or remove weights until the cap floats vertically with the water level about halfway up the cap.

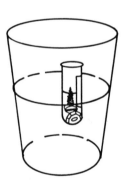

FIGURE 59-1. Lipstick cap floating vertically with nails showing.

5. Mark the water level on the cap.
6. Your cap is now a hydrometer. Hydrometers are used for measuring density of liquids, comparing them with the density of water. If the density is greater than that of water, the cap will float higher. If the density is less than that of water, the cap will sink deeper.
7. Dissolve about ¼ cup of salt in your jar of water. Without changing the number of weights in the cap, put it in the salt water. Does your hydrometer float deeper than it did in plain water or does it float higher? What does this tell you about the density of salt water?
8. Test other liquids, such as milk, vinegar, and rubbing alcohol.
9. As you test various liquids, make a list of those you think have a greater density than water has, and those that have a lesser density.

## TEACHER INFORMATION

Any object that floats displaces an amount of liquid equal to its own weight (Archimedes principle). If the specific gravity (density) of the liquid is greater, the object floats higher, since it has to displace less liquid to equal its own weight. If the hydrometer floats deeper, it is in a liquid of lower density.

Hydrometers are used to test such liquids as antifreeze and battery acid, using the Archimedes principle.

It is easier for swimmers to float in ocean water than in fresh water. Salt increases the density of water. Swimmers bob like a cork in the Great Salt Lake because of extremely high salt content. If salt water gets in the eyes, it will burn. A shower following the swim is necessary, as a film of salt is left on the skin after the water evaporates.

# ACTIVITY 60: How Does Temperature Affect the Speed of Molecules?

## MATERIALS NEEDED

- Two clear glasses
- Food coloring
- Paper and pencil

- Two eye droppers
- Hot water
- Cold water

## PROCEDURE

1. Put very cold water in one tumbler and hot water in the other. Fill each about half full.
2. Draw four or five drops of food coloring into each of the two eye droppers. Put as near the same amount in each as possible.
3. Hold a dropper over each tumbler and squeeze to empty the contents of both at exactly the same time.
4. Compare the movement of the color in the two containers. In which tumbler did the color spread more rapidly?
5. If you have time, try different colors and different water temperatures. Record your observations.

## TEACHER INFORMATION

As temperatures increase, molecules move faster. The food coloring should diffuse noticeably more rapidly in the hot water than in the cold water. In this activity, water temperature is the variable. You might have students try the same activity with color as the variable. For instance, use two tumblers of cold water and put red in one and green (or blue) in the other.

You might also consider having students use a stopwatch and a thermometer and record the actual time required for maximum diffusion (equal color throughout, as judged by the student).

# ACTIVITY 61: What Happens When Water Changes to a Solid?

(Teacher-supervised activity)

## MATERIALS NEEDED

- Two pint-sized glass jars
- One jar lid that seals
- Plastic ice tray
- Medicine or spice jar with pop-off (not safety) cap
- Water
- Freezer compartment
- Heavy cloth (dish towel)

## PROCEDURE

1. Completely fill both jars, the ice tray, and the small bottle with water.
2. Screw the cap tightly on one jar.
3. Wrap the jar with the lid in cloth.
4. Place all four containers upright in the freezer compartment. Leave for 24 hours.
5. Carefully unwrap the cloth from the jar.
6. Examine and compare the four containers.
7. What has happened to the water?
8. Can you explain the reason for the condition of each container?

## TEACHER INFORMATION

Unlike other material, water expands as it approaches the freezing point. The water in the open jar will be frozen, but the jar will be intact since the top was left open to permit expansion. The surface of the ice tray may be rippled showing a pattern first of expansion, then of contraction as the water became frozen. The jar wrapped in the cloth will be cracked and broken or the lid will be bulged or forced off. The top will be pushed off the small bottle.

Because water expands as it freezes, water-cooled engines require a coolant with a lower freezing point (antifreeze) in cold climates. Most engines also have "freeze plugs," which are designed to pop out, just like the top of the small bottle, to prevent serious damage to the engine. Outside water pipes are usually turned off and drained during winter months in cold climates.

# ACTIVITY 62:  How Can You Make a Worm?

## *MATERIALS NEEDED*

- Soda straw with sealed paper wrapper intact
- Water

- Medicine dropper
- Small dish

## *PROCEDURE*

1. Tear the top off the paper wrapper of a soda straw so the top of the straw can be seen.
2. Put the bottom of the straw on a table and carefully slide the paper wrapper down the straw until it is wrinkled, but no more than 5 cm. (2 in.) long.
3. Place the wrinkled "worm" on a small dish and use your medicine dropper to put three or four drops of water along its back.
4. What happened? What can you say about this?

Straw

Medicine dropper
Paper cover
Dish

FIGURE 62-1. Straw, paper wrapper, dish, and medicine dropper.

## *TEACHER INFORMATION*

When a few drops of water are put on the wrinkled paper, the "worm" will begin to grow and sometimes crawl. This is because the water spreads through the dry compressed paper and causes it to relax and expand.

Capillary action, of which this is one example, is the attraction or repulsion of liquids to solids. The study of surface tension in physics and chemistry and the science of chromatics also involve principles of capillary action. See your encyclopedia for further information. This is an excellent "take-home-and-talk-about" activity.

# Section 4

---

# WEATHER

# TO THE TEACHER

Weather is crucial in our lives. It influences where we live, what (and if) we eat, what we wear, what we do, and, sometimes, how we feel. Weather appears as a part of the first recorded history of man. Early civilizations grew and developed in favorable climates. The history of man is interwoven with myths, legends, stories, customs, religious beliefs, poems, art, music, dancing, and many other expressions that tell the story of man's continuing concern with the mysteries, beauties, and dangers of the often unpredictable nature of weather.

Today, sophisticated weather instruments circle the earth to report weather conditions on a global scale. Countless weather stations, with both professional and amateur meteorologists, study and report on a daily basis, yet frequently the news carries a report of some unpredicted or unusual occurrence. This section should help students understand some of the many variables that must be taken into account in a study of weather and to appreciate its importance in our lives.

This study draws heavily on information from the "Air" section and should follow it as closely as possible. You may even see a need to repeat some of the activities from the "Air" section.

Several activities require simple construction. Please take time to read *all* the activities before you begin. Parents and other resource people can be a great help in gathering and assisting as you build a weather station and a convection box. Be sure to plan to construct several of each of them.

If you teach young children, you will probably want to modify the weather chart and symbols. Activities 77 and 78 should be omitted.

Using the weather station and other sources to predict weather should take two to four weeks. However, it should not require too much time each day, so another section could be undertaken at the same time.

We hope you will use poetry, stories, music, and art liberally throughout the study.

Finally, *please* don't blame the weather on the weather forecaster.

# ACTIVITY 63: How Can You Make a Thermometer?

## MATERIALS NEEDED

- Commercial thermometer
- Clear, thin plastic tubing 30 cm. (12 in.) long
- 1-hole rubber stopper or cork with hole drilled through center
- Warm water
- Red food coloring
- Flask or small-mouthed glass bottle (cough medicine, etc.)
- Straight coat-hanger wire 30 cm. (12 in.) long
- 3" × 5" index card
- Candle wax or sealing wax (optional)

## PROCEDURE

1. The first thing most people notice about weather is the temperature. Thermometers, which tell temperature, are easy to make. You might have learned from activities in "Starter Ideas" and "Air" that liquids expand when they are heated and contract when they are cooled.
2. Fill the bottle with warm water. Add several drops of red food coloring.
3. Insert the plastic tube through the stopper or cork and fit the stopper tightly in the bottle. (If you use a cork, you may need to use candle wax or sealing wax to seal the opening between the tubing and the hole in the cork.) Water should be forced into the tube as you press the stopper into place.
4. Insert the coat-hanger wire through the tube for support.

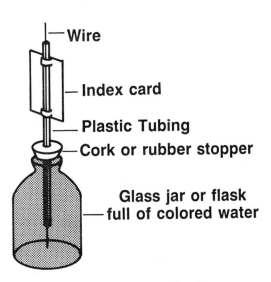

FIGURE 63.1. Homemade bottle thermometer.

5. Adjust the water level so the water will rise nearly halfway up the tube.
6. Make a slit near the bottom of the index card and another near the top and slide it behind the tube.
7. Wait about an hour for the water to reach room temperature.
8. Consult the commercial thermometer and mark the present temperature with a line on the index card.
9. Each morning and afternoon, compare the commercial thermometer with the one you have made. Make new lines to show changes.

## TEACHER INFORMATION

Ordinary methyl alcohol (or rubbing alcohol) may be substituted for water if the thermometer is to be left outside in below-freezing temperatures. **CAUTION: Methyl alcohol is poisonous if taken internally.**

The water expands because the molecules move more rapidly and push against each other as they are heated. As water cools, the molecules move more slowly and require less space, so the water contracts. This same principle is demonstrated with air several times in Section 2.

*Note:* Sealing wax will work better than candle wax because it remains flexible. Although candle wax hardens, it works reasonably well and is usually readily available.

# ACTIVITY 64: How Can You Make Another Kind of Thermometer?

## *MATERIALS NEEDED*

- The materials used in Activity 63
- Masking tape
- Small bowl
- Milk carton cut as support (see Figure 64-1)

## *PROCEDURE*

1. Insert the plastic tube in the cork or stopper just as you did in Activity 63.
2. Fit the cork in the bottle but do not add water.
3. Warm the jar by putting it near a heater or in warm water.
4. Fill the bowl with red colored water.
5. Place the bowl in the milk carton support.
6. Turn the warmed, empty jar upside down with the plastic tube all the way down in the bowl. You may need to use masking tape to hold the jar against the side of the carton.
7. Put an index card on the support behind the tube.
8. What happens as the warm jar cools to room temperature? Can you use information learned in the "Air" section to explain this?
9. Use a commercial thermometer to mark or calibrate your upside-down thermometer, just as you did in Activity 63.

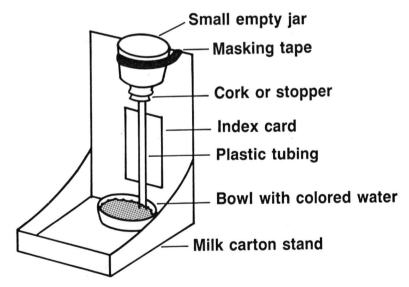

FIGURE 64-1. Homemade milk carton stand thermometer.

## *TEACHER INFORMATION*

This thermometer uses expanding and contracting air instead of water. When it is first set up, the air in the bottle will gradually cool and contract, reducing the pressure inside. Pressure on the surface of the colored water in the bowl will force liquid up the plastic tube.

This type of thermometer is usually less accurate than the upright kind because the air pressure pushing on the surface of the colored water varies according to the barometric pressure.

Measuring barometric pressure is the next activity.

# ACTIVITY 65: How Can We Measure Air Pressure?

(Teacher-supervised activity)

## *MATERIALS NEEDED*

- Wide-mouthed 1-quart glass jar
- Round balloon
- String or thick rubber band
- Commercial barometer
- Straw or broom straw
- Index card
- Milk carton cut into a stand
- Glue
- Scissors
- Pencil

## *PROCEDURE*

1. Cut the narrow neck off a balloon and stretch the balloon very tightly over the mouth of the glass jar.
2. Hold the balloon in place by wrapping and tying string below the threads of the jar.
3. Glue the straw to the center of the balloon in a horizontal position.
4. Attach the index card to the horizontal stand and bring it near the balloon.
5. Make a mark on the index card in the place where the straw points.
6. Consult your commercial barometer or call the local weather station to determine today's barometric pressure. Write the number beside the mark on your index card.
7. Repeat steps 5 and 6 every day for a week. What is happening? Discuss this with your teacher and class.

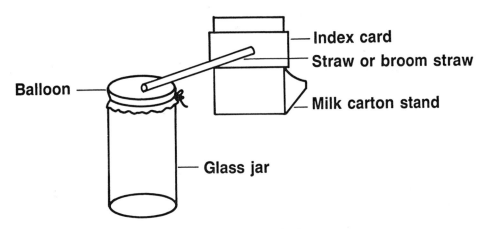

FIGURE 65-1. Homemade barometer.

## *TEACHER INFORMATION*

Close supervision for safety reasons is recommended because of the use of the glass jar, which could cause injury if broken.

Before discussing the barometer, you may want to remind the students of the air pressure activities in the section on air. Atmospheric pressure varies and is one indicator of weather conditions. Generally, lower barometric pressures accompany storm fronts, while higher pressures indicate fair weather.

When the balloon is stretched tightly over the bottle, the pressure inside the bottle will be the same as that of the atmosphere in the room. (Be careful not to force extra air trapped in the balloon into the bottle.) As the atmospheric pressure increases or decreases, it will change the amount of pressure on the balloon and cause the straw to move up or down. Because some air will pass through the balloon diaphragm, the air should be balanced by untying and retying the balloon about every three days.

Air temperature should be kept constant, as changes will affect comparative readings.

# ACTIVITY 66: How Can We Measure Moisture in the Air?

## *MATERIALS NEEDED*

- Empty half-gallon milk carton with the top cut off
- Drinking straw
- Small metal washer
- 5″ × 7″ index card
- Freshly washed human hair 20 cm. (8 in.) long
- Pins and thumbtacks
- Glass bead with hole
- Glue
- Ruler
- Toothpick
- Pencil

## *PROCEDURE*

1. Stick a pin through the end of the drinking straw and then through the bead. Near one edge of the carton, measure up from the bottom 10 cm. (4 in.) and stick the pin into the carton.
2. Reach inside the carton and put glue around the pin to hold it firmly in place. (The back from a pierced earring or tie pin may be used instead of glue.)
3. Attach the small metal washer to the straw just beyond the opposite edge of the carton.
4. Use a pin or thumbtack and glue to attach the hair to the top of the carton near the same edge as the washer. Tie and glue the hair to the straw at a point directly below.
5. Use two thumbtacks to attach the index card to the carton so it extends beyond the length of the straw. Glue a toothpick in the end of the straw as a pointer.
6. When you finish, your model should look like Figure 66-1.

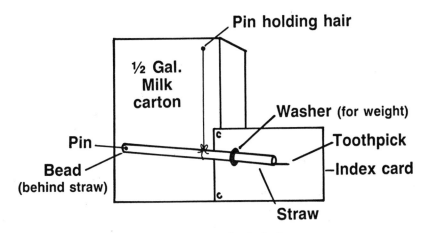

FIGURE 66-1. Homemade hair hygrometer.

7. This is a hair hygrometer. Make a pencil mark on the index card where the end of the straw is pointing.
8. In the next activity, you will learn how to use this and another kind of hygrometer to measure the moisture or humidity in the air.

## *TEACHER INFORMATION*

Hair absorbs moisture and becomes longer in humid air. In dry air, the hair contracts. The straw with the bead behind it, acting as a bearing, moves up and down, depending on the changes in length of the hair attached to it and the top of the milk carton. The washer attached to the straw provides extra weight and can be eliminated if the straw moves up and down without it. The toothpick and index card will make small movements easier to measure.

Be sure to make several hygrometers using different colors and textures of clean hair. If there are differences, your encyclopedia can tell you why.

# ACTIVITY 67: What Can Evaporation Tell Us About Humidity?

## MATERIALS NEEDED

- Two identical commercial thermometers (either Fahrenheit or Celsius)
- Shoelace (with tips cut off) 20 cm. (8 in.) long
- Two rubber bands
- Board 30 cm. (12 in.) long × 15 cm. (6 in.) wide
- Small glass full of water at room temperature

## PROCEDURE

1. Use the rubber bands to fasten the two thermometers side by side on the board about 10 cm.. (4 in.) apart.
2. Moisten the shoelace and wrap one end around the bulb of one thermometer. Put the other end of the shoelace in the glass of water.
3. After several minutes, compare the temperature of the thermometers.
4. What happened? Can you think of a way to explain this? Discuss this with your teacher and the class.

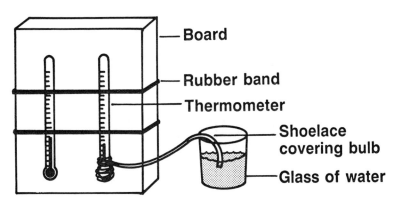

FIGURE 67-1. A wet-dry bulb hygrometer..

## TEACHER INFORMATION

After a few minutes, the wet bulb will have a lower temperature. This instrument is called a wet-dry bulb hygrometer. Meterologists (weather experts) often whirl wet and dry thermometers together in the air. The handle and instrument containing the thermometers, together are called a *sling psychrometer*. Your hygrometer works the same way, but not as rapidly. Students will often assume that the water is colder than the air and is making the wet bulb cooler. Actually, it is being cooled by the evaporation of moisture into the air.

Humidity is usually reported in percents. One hundred percent is the total amount of moisture air can contain. The less moisture the air contains, the greater the amount it can absorb. As the ability to absorb water increases, the temperature drops in a direct ratio. Therefore, the greater the difference in temperature between the wet and dry bulbs, the lower the humidity (amount of moisture already in the air).

The next activity compares the hair hygrometer and the wet-dry bulb.

# ACTIVITY 68: How Can You Compare the Wet-Dry Bulb and Hair Hygrometers?

## *MATERIALS NEEDED*

- Hygrometers from Activities 66 and 67
- Empty aquarium or large cardboard box lined with plastic garbage bags
- Pan of hot water
- Warm, moist bath towel
- Paper
- Pencil

## *PROCEDURE*

1. Mark the position of the straw on the index card of the hair hygrometer.
2. Compare and record the temperatures and difference in the wet-dry bulb hygrometer.
3. Put an open pan of hot water in the aquarium or box.
4. Carefully lower the hair hygrometer into the box and cover the top with the warm, moist towel. What do you think is happening inside the container? Can you predict what will happen to the hygrometers?
5. After waiting five minutes, gently remove the hygrometer from the box and on the index card mark the place where the straw is pointing.
6. Repeat steps 3, 4, and 5 exactly, using the wet-dry bulb hygrometer, except at the end, record the temperatures and the difference between them.
7. What kind of environment (conditions) did you create inside the container?
8. What can you say about the reactions of your hygrometers?

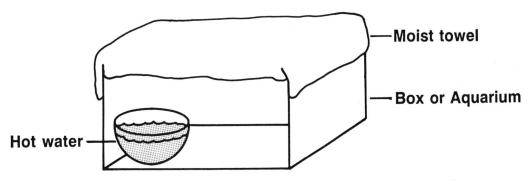

FIGURE 68-1. Aquarium with pan of water and moist towel.

## *TEACHER INFORMATION*

If possible, do this on a "normal" day for your climate. The pan of hot water and moist towel will create a very humid environment. The hair should lengthen and show a measurable difference on the card. The temperature of the wet bulb thermometer should increase more than that of the dry bulb, with little difference (both will go up some). The normal readings at the beginning of the activity, plus the moist reading at the end, should give students the beginning of a scale upon which they can record daily "readings" of the humidity.

# ACTIVITY 69: How Can You Tell Wind Direction?

(Teacher-supervised activity)

## *MATERIALS NEEDED*

- Two strips of heavy cardboard 45 cm. (18 in.) long × 15 cm. (6 in.) wide
- One piece of wood 15 cm. × 15 cm. (6 in. × 6 in.) and 3 cm. (1 in.) thick
- One piece of wood 5 cm. × 5 cm. (2 in. × 2 in.) and 20 cm. (8 in.) long
- Pencil
- Utility knife or scissors
- Awl (optional)
- Glass portion of medicine dropper or very thin glass bottle of about the same size
- One eight-penny finishing nail
- Strong glue
- Waterproof paint
- Paintbrush
- Meter stick

## *PROCEDURE*

1. You are going to construct an instrument to help chart wind direction.
2. On one strip of cardboard, draw an arrow with a small point, thin shaft, and wide tail.
3. With a utility knife or scissors, cut the first arrow out and use it as a pattern to make a second arrow. Glue the two arrows together.
4. To find the exact center, balance the arrow across the edge of a meter stick. Put a mark at that point.
5. Use a pointed object (pencil or awl) to make a hole through the shaft of the arrow at the balance point and glue the medicine dropper or bottle in it. This is the bearing upon which the arrow will turn.
6. Stand the 20-cm. (8-in.)-long piece of wood on end in the center of the 15-cm.- (6-in.)-square base and glue it in place.
7. Make a hole in the top center of the 20-cm. (8-in.) piece of wood and glue an eight-penny nail (point up) in it.
8. Put the glass bearing in the arrow over the nail in the base. The arrow should turn freely in all directions.
9. When the glue has dried, use waterproof paint on everything but the glass bearing and nail.
10. When finished, your weather instrument should look like Figure 69-1.

## *TEACHER INFORMATION*

Close supervision for safety reasons is recommended because of the use of glass, and of sharp objects, which could cause injury if broken or used carelessly.

To make the arrow, a single strip of plywood may be used if it is cut and balanced, and a hole is drilled in the center by heating it over a candle or alcohol lamp. **(CAUTION: Do not let students do this.)** Be sure to use very strong glue.

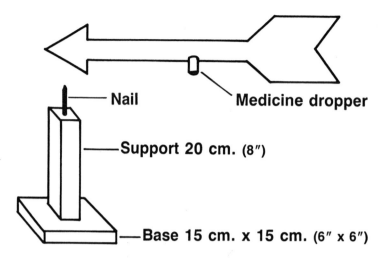

FIGURE 69-1. Homemade weather vane.

Weather vanes have been popular for centuries. Often they are beautiful intricately designed works of art used to decorate barns, houses, churches, and public buildings. A rooster perched on top is the most common identifying characteristic. A collection of pictures of elaborate weather vanes would make an attractive bulletin board display.

Tubular pieces of cloth called *windsocks* are often used at small airports. They are designed to turn in the direction of the wind and fill as the speed increases. As an enrichment activity, a windsock could be constructed from a coat hanger frame and a nylon stocking with the foot cut out.

*Note:* Activity 71 requires the materials used in this activity to construct support bases. As you prepare materials for Activity 69, cut extra square bases and support columns for Activity 71.

# ACTIVITY 70: How Can You Use a Weather Vane?

## *MATERIALS NEEDED*

- 30 sheets of paper 30 cm. × 30 cm. (12 in. × 12 in.)
- Weather vane from Activity 69
- Directional compass
- Ruler
- Pencil

## *PROCEDURE*

1. Measure down 15 cm. (6 in.) on each edge of your paper and draw lines that will divide it into quarters.
2. Draw straight lines through the center to opposite corners of your paper.
3. Put the ruled paper under the directional compass. Locate magnetic north and turn your paper so the line on one edge points north. Write an N on that line and fill in the rest of your chart as shown in Figure 70-1.
4. Ask your teacher to make 30 additional copies of your diagram so you can keep future records.
5. Go outside and find an open area where the wind blows in all directions. Use the compass to determine north, align your paper properly, and put your weather vane on it.
6. Return to the same place and repeat step 5 four times a day. Each time, draw a line to mark the time of day and the wind direction on your sheet. Do this for 30 days.

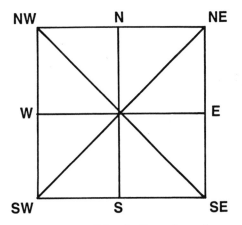

FIGURE 70-1. Wind direction chart.

## *TEACHER INFORMATION*

Depending on your climate and the time of year, wind direction may not change frequently. Twice a day may be sufficient to obtain the necessary information. Wind direction will be combined with data from the other instruments to develop a student-made weather station.

# ACTIVITY 71: How Can Wind Speed Be Measured?

(Teacher-supervised activity)

## MATERIALS NEEDED

- Materials used in Activity 69 to construct a support base
- Two strips of lath 40 cm. (16 in.) long
- One piece of coat-hanger wire 20 cm. (8 in.) long
- Four 4-ounce paper cups
- File
- Thumbtacks
- Glass medicine dropper or very thin glass bottle
- Strong glue
- Small 2 cm. (¾ in.) nails
- Hammer
- Drill
- Brightly colored paint
- Paintbrush
- Thin tie wire

## PROCEDURE

1. Find the middle of each lath, make them into the shape of a cross, and glue them together. Use four small nails to hold them securely.
2. Have your teacher drill a hole in the exact center of the cross large enough to accommodate the medicine dropper or bottle.
3. Construct a supporting base as shown in Activity 70, but do not use an eight-penny nail on top. Instead, file one end of the coat-hanger wire to a point. Use the tie wire to securely bind the coat-hanger wire, point up, to the upright column of the base.
4. Glue a 4-ounce paper cup to each of the four ends of the cross. Use thumbtacks, too, for extra strength. Be sure the open ends of all the cups face in the same direction. Paint one cup a bright color.
5. Put the medicine dropper in the cross over the pointed wire in the support base. When completed, the cross and cups should spin freely.
6. This instrument is called an *anemometer* (see Figure 71-1), and it is used to measure wind speed.

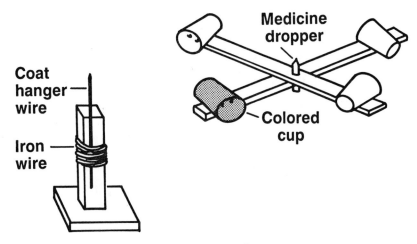

FIGURE 71-1. Homemade anemometer.

## TEACHER INFORMATION

It is very important that the anemometer be balanced and spin freely. If medicine droppers are used, they should be prepared in advance. A parent or aide could be enlisted to use a hand drill to bore the holes in the cross pieces.

The next activity will help students use the anemometer to measure wind speed fairly accurately.

# ACTIVITY 72: How Does an Anemometer Work?

(Do this in moderate wind)

## *MATERIALS NEEDED*

- Anemometer constructed in Activity 71
- Stopwatch or watch with second hand
- Paper
- Pencil
- Masking tape

## *PROCEDURE*

1. Take the materials to an open area outside where the wind can blow in all directions.
2. Put the anemometer on a flat surface where it will spin freely. Put a strip of masking tape on the flat surface under the cups so they will pass over it each time they spin around.
3. Use the colored cup as a counter and mark each time it passes over the strip during a 60-second period.
4. Divide the number of times the colored cup passes over the strip by ten and you will have the approximate speed of the wind.
5. Repeat steps 1-4 each day at the same time the weather vane is checked. Keep a record of the date, time, and wind speed for 30 days.

## *TEACHER INFORMATION*

Friction will be an important factor in the accuracy of the anemometer. You can calibrate the accuracy to some degree if on a very calm day you hold the anemometer out the window of a car at various speeds while timing the number of spins. If the car is driven for one minute at 5, 10, and 15 miles per hour, you should have enough data to compare with the stationary recordings. The anemometer must be held far enough away from the car so air currents caused by the car do not disturb it.

# ACTIVITY 73: How Can Rainfall Be Measured?

(Rain is needed for this activity)

## *MATERIALS NEEDED*

- Straight-sided water glass or pan at least 20 cm. (8 in.) tall
- Ruler or meter stick
- Paper
- Pencil

## *PROCEDURE*

1. When rain is expected, take the can or glass outside to a place where there are no buildings, walls, trees, or other obstructions nearby.
2. As soon as possible after the rain stops, use the ruler to measure the amount of water in the container.
3. Rainfall is usually reported in inches or centimeters.
4. Keep a chart for 30 days listing the date and the amount of rain.
5. If you are studying weather at a time when most of the precipitation is snow, you can measure snow depth with the meter stick if you are in an open area.
6. If you are measuring precipitation in the form of snow, sleet, or hail, you can collect it in a wastebasket or pail, bring it into a warm place to melt and measure the water content. Different types of snow contain varying amounts of water per centimeter or inch.

## *TEACHER INFORMATION*

Some rain gauges use a funnel at the top of the collector. This may be helpful in collecting some wind-blown rain, but you should take into account the diameter of the funnel versus the diameter of the container and correct your measurement accordingly. Moisture content is very important in measuring snow. Five cm. (2 in.) of wet snow may contain more moisture than 20 cm. (8 in.) of powdery snow. If a slight amount of rain falls, but is not measurable, it should be recorded as a "trace."

# ACTIVITY 74: How Can You Operate a Weather Station?

(Class-planning activity)

## *MATERIALS NEEDED*

- 1¼-m. × 2-m. (4-ft. × 6-ft.) sheet of paper for bulletin board
- Meter stick
- Crayons
- Markers

## *PROCEDURE*

1. Now that you have instruments to record the weather, plan a 30-day chart to record it. Use the sample "Weather Chart" as a starting point. You will need to decide the data you want to record each day and assign committees to record it.
2. The Weather Bureau uses standard symbols to indicate weather conditions. Your teacher can help you get a book to let you learn to use these symbols if you care to. For example, the symbol for snow is ✱ ● means rain, ❟ means drizzle, and ↯ means thunderstorm. Perhaps you would rather make up your own symbols.
3. Leave four extra columns at the end to record weather reports from other sources and to record the actual weather. The next activity will explain how to obtain information from them.
4. In addition to the large bulletin board chart, you may want to make smaller copies for your own use.

## *TEACHER INFORMATION*

Use a rectangular shape for your weather chart. The sizes of the columns and the symbols listed along the left side are suggestions. The official Weather Bureau symbols are much more complicated and usually unnecessary to use for a short period of time. The chart in the example provides for 15 days. This is a minimum recommended time for the study. Thirty days would provide for a more accurate comparison. Daily readings should take only a few minutes, so other science projects could be planned for the remaining time.

# Weather Chart

| Key ✳ | | | | | | | | | | Tomorrow's Forecast | | | | Today's Actual Weather |
|---|---|---|---|---|---|---|---|---|---|---|---|---|---|---|
| Symbol | Condition | Date | Time | Temp | Wind Speed | Wind Direction | Humidity | Air Pressure | Class | Commercial | Weather Bureau TV, Radio, News | Farmers Almanac | | |
| ◯ | Clear Sky | | | | | | | | | | | | | |
| ◑ | Partly Cloudy | | | | | | | | | | | | | |
| ⬤ | Rain | | | | | | | | | | | | | |
| ✳ | Snow | | | | | | | | | | | | | |
| ↰ | Thunder Storm | | | | | | | | | | | | | |
| ◗ | Drizzle | | | | | | | | | | | | | |
| ≡ | Fog | | | | | | | | | | | | | |
| ☁ | Warm Front | | | | | | | | | | | | | |
| ⚡ | Cold Front | | | | | | | | | | | | | |
| ⟲ | Dust Storm | | | | | | | | | | | | | |
| ▷ | Showers | | | | | | | | | | | | | |
| ◁▷ | Hail | | | | | | | | | | | | | |
| ◁ | Sleet | | | | | | | | | | | | | |
| ◇ | Smoke | | | | | | | | | | | | | |
| ∞ | Haze | | | | | | | | | | | | | |

✳ (not an official key)

◐⬤ more symbols — stronger conditions

✳▷ symbol above symbol — mixed conditions

# ACTIVITY 75: What Is the Best Source for Predicting Weather

(Group activity)

## MATERIALS NEEDED

- Weather instruments constructed in previous activities
- Commercial weather instruments manufactured for home use
- *The Old Farmers Almanac*
- Pencil
- A single professional source for weather reporting, such as a newspaper, television, radio, or the United States Weather Bureau
- Weather chart from Activity 74

## PROCEDURE

1. Your teacher will tell you about four different methods you can use to predict weather. Choose one of the four and form a "weather team."
2. For the next several weeks, meet with your group, study the information you have collected from your source for the day and record your group's prediction of what tomorrow's weather will be on the chart.
3. At the end of the week, compare each of the four predictions with actual weather as it occurred. If your predictions were not accurate, try to think of ways to improve your predictions.

## TEACHER INFORMATION

The main objective of this activity is to help students become aware of the many factors that exist in any attempt to predict weather accurately.

Commercial weather instruments for home use are sold in many stores. They usually consist of a thermometer, aneroid barometer, and hygrometer. You can probably borrow a set from someone in your school community.

In selecting a professional source, try to locate an individual in the organization with whom you can work. This "weather person" can become an excellent resource and may be able to assist by providing materials and arranging field trips. If you make daily contact with an agency by telephone, be certain only one student is selected to make the call.

*The Old Farmers Almanac* is available at many bookstores and magazine outlets. It has been in continuous publication for nearly 200 years. The entire publication, including the ads and special articles, is informational and entertaining, and it provides fascinating insight into a segment of American society that is often overlooked today. According to the *Almanac*, its weather predictions are based on a secret formula devised by its founder, Robert B. Thomas, in 1792, and by the most modern scientific calculation based on solar activity. You may be interested in examining this publication for use in social studies teaching as well. It is highly recommended for your personal library.

Long-term predictions are not included in this activity. However, this would be an appropriate time to introduce the recent use of technology such as weather satellites, international observatories, and cloud-seeding techniques to predict and influence the weather (see encyclopedia and books on weather from your library).

# ACTIVITY 76: What Are Some Unusual Ways to Predict and Explain Weather?

(A just-for-fun activity)

## MATERIALS NEEDED

- Books and stories
- Traditions and myths
- Older adults

## PROCEDURE

1. Groundhog Day is known and observed almost everywhere in the United States. Find out all you can about this special day and share with your class.
2. Below are listed a number of other ways people use to predict weather. How many do you know? Can you complete the sentences?

> Woolly caterpillars tell us _____.
>
> Amount of fur or fat on animals tells us _____.
>
> The Indians say _____.
>
> My grandmother's arthritis _____.
>
> My grandfather's corns _____.
>
> The animals (squirrels, birds, etc.) are _____.
>
> A ring around the moon means _____.
>
> "Red sky at night, sailors delight; red sky at morning, sailors take _____.
>
> A "rain dance" is _____.
>
> When north winds blow, _____.

3. Form a committee and find out as much as you can about folk methods for predicting and changing weather.
4. With your teacher's help, make an illustrated book on folk weather.

## *TEACHER INFORMATION*

Although it is not scientific, this activity may help children become aware of the many ways people have used to understand, predict, and influence the weather. Weather conditions in some manner influence many factors in our lives and, in fact, indirectly or directly determine our existence. Technology has enabled us to walk on the moon, circle the earth in an hour, see an event as it happens anywhere on earth—yet we are all at the mercy of the weather, just as we were centuries ago.

In your book of folk weather, be sure to include songs, poems, stories, and pictures to portray the feelings of mystery, power, beauty, wonder, and awe of that remarkable phenomenon we call weather.

Finally, remember the old saying, "It always rains on the weathermen's picnic."

# ACTIVITY 77: How Do Heating and Cooling Affect Air Currents?

(Teacher-supervised activity)

## *MATERIALS NEEDED*

- 10-gallon aquarium and sheet of cardboard to cover the top *or* a cardboard box approximately the same size
- Two glass lamp chimneys
- Large cup or small pan
- Incense or hemp rope to produce smoke
- Roll of 5-cm. (2-in.)-wide plastic tape
- Drawing compass

- Transparent plastic wrap if a cardboard box is used instead of an aquarium
- Match
- Small bowls
- Hot water
- Warm water
- Very cold water
- Knife or scissors

## *PROCEDURE*

1. If the aquarium is used, fit the cardboard covering snugly on top.
2. Measure the diameter of the bottom of a lamp chimney and use the compass to make a circle near each end of the cardboard top.
3. Cut out the circles and fit a lamp chimney in each.
4. If you use a cardboard box, cut off the top flaps and use the plastic wrap to make a window. Seal the wrap and all other openings in the box with plastic tape. Lay the box on its side and make holes in the top for lamp chimneys as explained in steps 2 and 3. In one end of the box, cut a door that can be opened and closed.
5. Whether you use an aquarium or a cardboard box, seal any space around the lamp chimneys with plastic tape.
6. Light the incense or rope and put it in a large cup or small pan in the center of the box. Observe what happens.
7. Place a cup of warm water in the box under one lamp chimney. What happened?
8. Repeat steps 6 and 7 using very hot and very cold water.
9. Look in your window to observe what happens.
10. This is called a convection box. Using information you have learned about air, explain what happened.

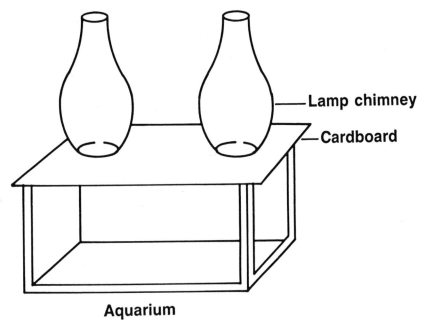

**Aquarium**

FIGURE 77-1. Aquarium with lamp chimneys in cardboard top.

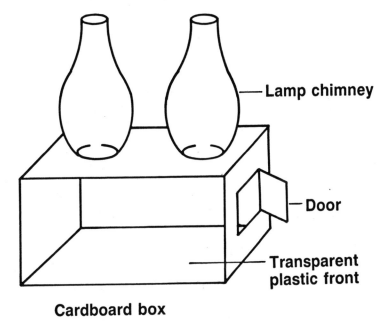

**Cardboard box**

FIGURE 77-2. Box with lamp chimneys and transparent side.

## *TEACHER INFORMATION*

Before you begin this activity, you may want to review concepts from the section on air. When warm water is placed under one of the lamp chimneys in the box, the air around it will be heated and rise. Cooler air will be drawn into the box through the other chimney. Smoke will clearly show the currents.

If you think of the bottom of the convection box as a large area of the earth's surface that heats and cools irregularly due to the shape and material (land, water) of its surface, perhaps you can visualize how large warm and cold air masses develop and cause constant movement of the air.

Each time the water is changed, the smoke should be exhausted from the box. When fresh smoke and a different temperature of water are used, allow several minutes for the atmosphere to change in the box.

# ACTIVITY 78: What Can We Learn from a Convection Box?

(Upper-grade activity)

## MATERIALS NEEDED

- Lamp chimney convection box from Activity 77
- Two sheets of 9" × 12" newsprint
- Pencil
- Large cups
- Smoke source
- Hot water
- Cold water

## PROCEDURE

1. Study the convection box and draw a picture of it.
2. Use hot water and smoke to start air movement in the real convection box.
3. Since we know that faster-moving air has lower pressure, where might a difference in air pressure be inside your box? Write "high" and "low" in the places where you think the pressures might be different.
4. Since we know warm air can hold more moisture than cold air, where might the differences in humidity be inside your box? Write "moist" and "dry" where you think the air contains more and less humidity..

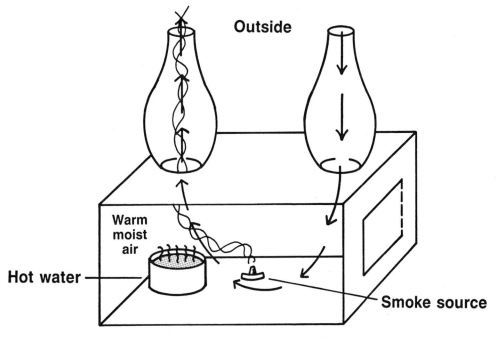

FIGURE 78-1. Convection box with hot water.

5. Draw another picture of the convection box.
6. Replace the hot water with ice water in the actual box.
7. Observe the behavior of the smoke. Repeat steps 3 and 4, marking the places in the box where you think air pressure and humidity might differ.
8. Under what conditions does the air (wind) move faster?

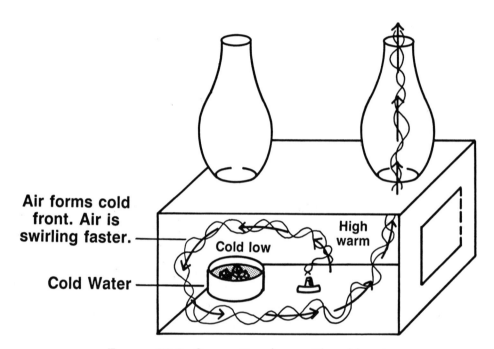

**Air forms cold front. Air is swirling faster.**

**Cold low**

**Cold Water**

**High warm**

FIGURE 78-2. Convection box with cold water.

## TEACHER INFORMATION

The students should not see Figures 78-1 and 78-2 until they have completed the activity. Although it would require very sensitive instruments to measure the differences, they do occur.

Some students may have difficulty with the abstract thinking this activity requires. A class discussion and review at the end of the activity should help.

This activity may also help you determine how well children understand the basic principles of weather and air that have been developed up to this point.

The next activities will use these basic concepts to make generalizations about the causes of weather regionally and worldwide.

# ACTIVITY 79: What Makes Rain?

## *MATERIALS NEEDED*

- One profile weather picture for each student
- Paper
- Pencil

## *PROCEDURE*

1. Study Figure 79-1. Can you see the relationships?
2. Write a story that describes what is happening from left to right in the picture. Can you explain why?

## *TEACHER INFORMATION*

This is a simplified diagram of one way weather can change. Reading from left to right: Sun shines on water, causing it to warm and evaporate. The air above is warm and moist and rises until it reaches the upper atmosphere and begins to cool. As it cools, moisture condenses and clouds begin to form. Prevailing winds that move from water to land carry the clouds inland, where they continue to pick up moisture.

When the clouds reach the mountain, they are forced upward into cooler air. As the air in the clouds cools rapidly, it must reduce its moisture content, which it does at lower elevations in the form of rain and at higher elevations in the form of snow.

After clouds are forced up by a high mountain range, they may give up enough moisture so less precipitation falls on the far side of the mountain. This area is called a *rain shadow.*

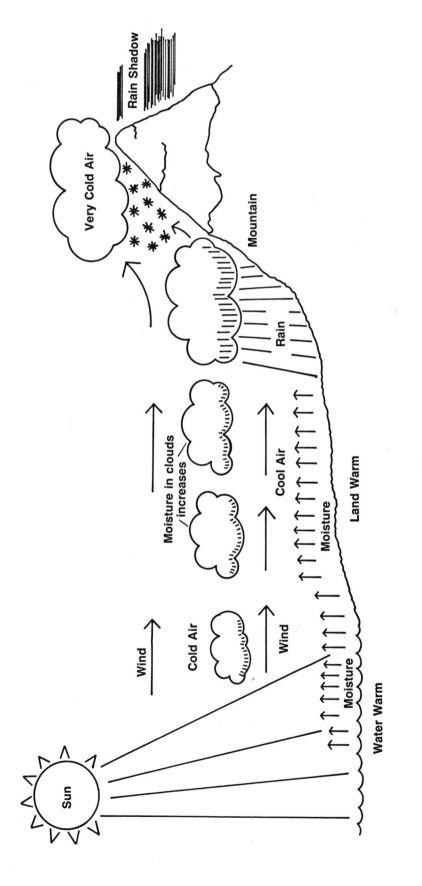

FIGURE 79-1. Profile of water, land, and mountains.

# ACTIVITY 80: What Is a Cold Front?

## *MATERIALS NEEDED*

- One copy of Figure 80-1 for each student
- Crayons

## *STUDENT INFORMATION*

If all weather patterns were as simple as the one shown in Activity 89, the weather forecaster's job would be easy. Actually, different air masses form over water, ice, and dry land. Many different kinds of air masses are moving over the earth at different altitudes at the same time. When they collide, they often do not mix. At the point of impact, weather disturbances, sometimes of unpredictable extent, occur. The picture shows what can happen when cold and warm air masses collide.

## *PROCEDURE*

1. Study the picture of colliding air masses. In this case, the cold air mass is somewhat like a moving mountain. Use your red crayon to write "warm" where you think warm temperatures would be found.
2. Use a blue crayon to write "cold" and "very cold" where you think cold temperatures might occur.
3. Use a green crayon to write "moist" where the most humidity will be found.
4. Use a yellow crayon to write "dry" where you think there is less moisture.
5. Use a black crayon to write "high" or "low" where you think air pressure differences might occur.
6. Compare and discuss your picture with your teacher and other members of the class.

## *TEACHER INFORMATION*

The temperature will be warmer near the ground in the area before the approaching front. Temperatures behind and above the front will be colder.

As the cold front pushes the warm air upward, precipitation may occur. The type of precipitation will depend on the temperature of the air. The common weather prediction of "rain turning to snow" tells the progress of the cold front.

Because cold fronts move faster, the air pressure will be lower behind the front.

The humidity will be greater in areas before and following the front line.

If the cold front should stop over the town, it would be called *stationary*. Stationary lows and highs often determine weather for long periods of time over large regions of the country.

Occasionally, especially in mountainous areas, a cold front may become stationary with a warm air mass above it. The warm air forms a blanket and retards circulation of the cold air. This is called a *temperature inversion*. If a temperature inversion occurs over a city, air does not circulate and smog will develop.

If you live in an area near a large body of water, such as an ocean or gulf, your weather is controlled to a great extent by the water mass. Since the air temperature over water does not change as much as it does over land, your temperatures could vary less. Latitude and ocean currents will be of greater importance. Severe storms will most often develop over the body of water and move onto land, especially in the southern latitudes. Weather is also greatly influenced by large lakes, rivers, mountains, and valleys.

A final evaluation for this study could be to have the students draw, label, and explain a picture of the last storm that occurred in their area.

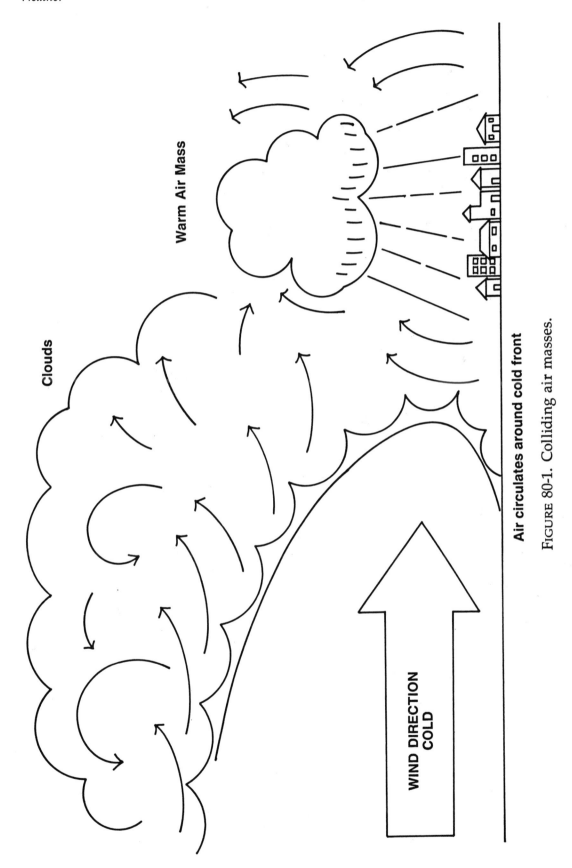

**Clouds**

**Warm Air Mass**

**WIND DIRECTION COLD**

**Air circulates around cold front**

FIGURE 80-1. Colliding air masses.

# Section 5

---

# THE EARTH

# TO THE TEACHER

We live on a combination of rock, soil, and water known as the earth's crust. We depend on this relatively thin layer (along with air and sunlight) to provide our food, medicine, and clothing—and the materials to build our homes, cars, and other things. Geologists continually search the earth's surface for clues to the location of mineral resources and answers to questions about the origin, early history, and current changes of the surface of this planet. A study of its structure and evolutionary history helps to increase our appreciation for the earth and its resources.

Scientists are interested in the composition of the earth, the forces that shape and change it, and how it came to be as it is. From a career point of view, exposure to some of these ideas can help students begin to develop a perception of geology-related occupations and even stimulate possible early interests. From the standpoint of general interest, horizons are broadened within the mind as students acquire a glimpse of the significance and majesty of this great planet.

The first several activities of this unit are map oriented. The objective of these activities is not to present a thorough treatment of map reading, but to develop the concept of representing the earth, or small portions of it, on paper or other surface that can be used for observation and study. The map-related questions in this section deal with the problems arising from efforts to represent size and shape in miniature form. Even in the very early grades, students can begin forming concepts about the earth's magnitude and structure.

Children are natural collectors. This interest can be stimulated and broadened by encouraging them to watch for new kinds of rocks; then provide simple ideas for recognizing likenesses and differences in rocks they find and categorizing them according to those recognized attributes.

Along with involvement in the activities of this section, emphasis should be placed on appropriate geologic concepts. The earth's crust, for instance, consists largely of rock layers that have been formed and layered by such factors as heat, pressure, and the effects of water and cementing material. Under the earth's crust is molten rock, called *magma*. Great pressures sometimes force magma to the surface, forming volcanoes. Other forces shift the outer layers of the earth's surface, causing earthquakes and forming mountains and valleys, sometimes causing much destruction in life and property.

Many locations are rich with nearby sites where geologic changes are evident—exposed rock layers on a mountainside or at an excavation site, a glacier-formed canyon, or a terrace that was once the beach of an ancient lake. These examples and many more stand as evidence of the ever-changing nature of the earth's surface. A geologist, forest ranger, or rock collector could provide fascinating information about local geologic interests.

Those living in the city are limited in availability of rocks for collection from natural settings, but a little creative effort can compensate rather well. Samples can be obtained from science supply catalogs or from local rock collectors. Possibly one or more students have collected rocks while on vacation that they would be pleased to bring to class and share with the group. As a group, the class might acquire an impressive rock collection by writing to friends and relatives. Trips to a local museum can provide meaningful geologic field trips.

# ACTIVITY 81: How Are Size and Distance Shown on a Map?

## MATERIALS NEEDED

- 8½" × 11" paper
- Ruler
- Pencil

## PROCEDURE

1. Draw a map of your classroom. Be sure to include the furnishings, such as tables, chairs, bookcases, and desks.
2. Look carefully at your map. Compare it with the classroom. Do they look the same? Are they the same size?
3. If you mailed your map to a friend, what could you do to help your friend understand how big the room and the pieces of furniture really are? If others are doing this same activity, talk to them about ideas for including this information on your map.
4. When you think of an answer to Step 3, fix your map so it will show how big things on it really are.

## TEACHER INFORMATION

A map is a representation of a portion of the earth, or sometimes all of it. This activity introduces a series of activities designed to help children understand how the earth, or portions of it, is represented in miniature form for observation and study. Depending upon maturity level and prior experience with maps, students might need assistance in deriving a suitable answer for the question in step 3. One solution is to use a scale, letting each centimeter or inch on the map represent a certain distance in the classroom. Any workable solution should be accepted. If those given are impractical, students can be led to "discover" the use of a scale through discussion and use.

# ACTIVITY 82: How Can You Show Your School Grounds on a Sheet of Paper?

---

## *MATERIALS NEEDED*

- 8½″ × 11″ paper
- Ruler
- Pencil

## *PROCEDURE*

1. In Activity 81, you drew a map of your classroom and furniture. If you followed the instructions carefully, you included a way for your map to show the real size of objects on it.
2. Draw a map of your school grounds, including the schoolhouse, ball field, playground, swings, and all other equipment. Before you begin, review what you did for Activity 81. Use the same idea for showing the real size of things on your school grounds map that you used on your classroom map.
3. Compare your school grounds map with your classroom map. What is the same and what is different?
4. On your map of the school grounds, draw your classroom in the school building, showing it in its actual location in the building.
5. Could you draw all the furniture in your classroom on this map, just as you did on your first map? What is different? Why?
6. What changes does a map maker have to make in order to show larger areas on a map?

## *TEACHER INFORMATION*

The purpose of this activity is to cause students to expand the amount of area they include as they draw a map on paper. They should begin to get the idea that any area can be represented on a small sheet of paper. As the area increases in size, the scale must change putting more actual distance into a given amount of space on the map. In discussion of steps 5 and 6, be sure students realize that the map maker must decrease detail as greater areas are represented.

# ACTIVITY 83: How Can a Flat Map Show Three Dimensions?

(Individual or small-group activity)

## MATERIALS NEEDED

- Clay
- Pencil
- Paper

## PROCEDURE

1. Form your clay into the shape of a mountain.
2. Now draw your mountain on paper. Think of a way to show the high and low places on your "map." If others are doing the same activity, talk about ways this could be done.
3. Use whatever idea you think is best to show the high and low places of your mountain on your map.

## TEACHER INFORMATION

The purpose of this activity is to help students discover ways to show a third dimension on a flat surface. This is commonly achieved with *relief* maps. Depending on maturity of students and prior experience with maps, they may or may not think to use shading or color coding. These methods could be suggested, but students should first be encouraged to devise their own ways to show the highs and lows of their mountain on paper. Original ideas that communicate the information, as well as the tried-and-true techniques, should be accepted and praised.

As a test of accuracy in their use of techniques for showing these dimensions, students might enjoy trading maps with a classmate. Each should leave his or her original mountain intact, get additional clay, and construct a second mountain from the borrowed map. Then each child should compare the second mountain with the classmate's original, to see how well the intended communication was interpreted.

# ACTIVITY 84: What Are Contour Lines?

## *MATERIALS NEEDED*

- Clay
- Pencil
- Paper
- Thick book
- Thin book

## *PROCEDURE*

1. Form your clay into the shape of a mountain. Include hills and valleys, steep slopes, and gradual slopes.
2. Lay a thick book on the table beside your "mountain."
3. Sight across the book to your mountain and put marks all the way around your mountain at the same level as the top of the book.
4. Draw a line around the mountain, connecting the marks you made for step 3.
5. Now stand above your mountain and look down at the line you drew. Does the line form a circle? What shape does it form? This is called a *contour line.*
6. Use a thinner book and draw a contour line further down the mountainside. Then stack two books and draw a contour line further up the mountainside. Draw still more contour lines if you wish, but keep them apart from each other.
7. Stand over your mountain and look down at the contour lines. Are they the same distance apart all the way around the mountain?
8. Draw your mountain on paper, including all contour lines as they appear from above. When you finish you will have a *contour map.*
9. Trade contour maps with a classmate. Look at your classmate's map and try to visualize what the mountain looks like. Then look at the actual mountain and see if you were right.

## *TEACHER INFORMATION*

The contour map is a very popular and practical way of illustrating elevation on a flat surface. This activity should add meaning to the next, as students try to interpret an actual contour map to determine the highs and lows and the gradual and steep slopes.

# ACTIVITY 85:  What Is a Contour Map?

## *MATERIALS NEEDED*

- Commercial contour maps
- Clay

## *PROCEDURE*

1. Examine your contour map. Your experience from Activity 85 should help you understand the lines on this map.
2. How much elevation (height) is represented from one contour line to the next?
3. Select one section of the map. Study it carefully and try to visualize the area it represents.
4. Make a clay model of this section of the map.
5. Trade maps with a classmate. Examine and evaluate each other's work.

## *TEACHER INFORMATION*

This activity can be done individually or in small groups. Before you begin, the previous activity should be reviewed. Any contour maps can be used, but if maps can be obtained that represent a local area familiar to students, the experience will be more meaningful. Students might need help in determining the *contour interval* (amount of elevation change represented from one contour line to the next).

If the maps used represent a local area, consider taking a field trip to that area. Students could then compare the maps with the actual terrain and evaluate their own interpretation of the map. If a class field trip is not possible, perhaps some students could take a field trip of their own, with the family or a group of friends.

If the class or group of students visits a local area with contour maps in hand, consider having them try to walk the contour lines for a distance. After determining the contour interval, each of several students could stand at the point best determined to be a contour line on the map. Then all in the group walk in unison around the terrain, being careful not to walk up or down the slope, each remaining as nearly as possible at the same elevation as the starting point. The vertical distance between participants should remain constant, but the horizontal distance should vary as they walk along the terrain, as it varies on the contour map.

# ACTIVITY 86: How High and Low Are the Earth's Mountains and Valleys?

## *MATERIALS NEEDED*

- World relief map or globe
- Pencil
- Paper

## *PROCEDURE*

1. Study your relief map until you know how to determine the elevations of the different areas.
2. Write down several of the highest elevations you can find. Include the name of the mountain each one represents and the country it is in.
3. Write down several of the lowest elevations you can find and the name of the area each represents.
4. How much higher are the highest points than the lowest points?
5. The distance through the earth is approximately 8,000 miles. Draw a circle to represent the earth and make a mark to show how high above the line the highest mountain would be. Show the lowest ocean floor also.
6. If others are doing this activity, compare notes and discuss your findings.

## *TEACHER INFORMATION*

Locating some of the highs and lows on the earth will help students visualize the earth. When they do step 5, some might be surprised to find that, although the distances to mountain peaks and ocean floors seem great, they actually represent very slight distortions on the earth's skin.

# ACTIVITY 87: How Can a Flat Map Represent the Earth?

(Teacher-supervised activity)

## *MATERIALS NEEDED*

- World relief globe
- World relief map
- Fresh orange
- Dull knife
- Pencil
- Paper

## *PROCEDURE*

1. Carefully remove the peel from your orange, keeping it all in one piece or in as large pieces as possible.
2. Try to lay the orange peel out flat on the paper. What happened?
3. Cut off a piece of orange peel about 2–3 cm. (1 in.) square and lay it out flat on your paper. Did that work any better?
4. On the globe, compare the size of the United States with the size of Greenland.
5. Now compare the same two countries on the flat map. What do you find?
6. Think about what you did with the orange peel in step 2. What problems do there seem to be with representing a ball-shaped object on a flat surface?
7. If you were a map maker, what would you do to show the earth on a flat map?

## *TEACHER INFORMATION*

In doing this activity, students should begin to understand the problems involved with representing the spherically shaped earth on a flat map. After students have struggled with the question in step 7, discuss the ideas that were produced. This would be an excellent time to discuss different types of projections used in mapmaking. Bring samples to class if possible. Consider having students try to make one or more of these with their orange peel (or a new one), by cutting along the "meridians," then flattening it out on paper. Discuss the advantages and disadvantages of the different types of projections.

# ACTIVITY 88: How Does the Nature of the Earth's Surface Affect Temperature?

## MATERIALS NEEDED

- Relief maps
- Temperature maps
- Paper
- Pencil

## PROCEDURE

1. Study your temperature maps and identify at least 10 areas that have high average temperatures.
2. Find these same areas on the relief map. Do they seem to be areas of high altitude, low altitude, medium altitude, or a mixture of all three?
3. Are these areas commonly near mountain ranges, near oceans, or far away from both—or does it seem to be a mixture?
4. Are these areas near the equator or nearer to the North Pole or South Pole?
5. Next, identify at least 10 areas that have low average temperatures. Do steps 2, 3, and 4 with them.
6. What can you say about the effect altitude has on temperature?
7. What effect do mountain ranges and oceans seem to have on temperature?
8. What effect does latitude (distance from the equator) have on temperature?

## TEACHER INFORMATION

Temperatures are affected by altitude. In general, the higher the altitude, the cooler the climate will be. Even near the equator, areas of higher altitude have cooler temperatures than do those near sea level. Oceans tend to have a moderating effect on nearby land masses, as water heats up and cools down more slowly than does land. Air masses coming from the oceans can have a great cooling or warming effect on temperature over land areas, depending upon whether they are coming from the cold arctic waters or from warmer ocean currents.

Latitude affects temperature more than any other single factor. Regions near the equator are said to have a low latitude. High latitudes are near the poles. The higher the latitude of a region, the colder the climate will be. Low latitudes get the direct rays of the sun. Higher latitudes get slanted, less concentrated rays.

# ACTIVITY 89: How Do Mountains Affect Yearly Rainfall?

## *MATERIALS NEEDED*

- Relief maps
- Rainfall maps
- Paper
- Pencil

## *PROCEDURE*

1. Study your rainfall maps and identify at least 10 areas that have high average rainfall.
2. Find these same areas on the relief map. Do they seem to be areas of high altitude, low altitude, medium altitude or a mixture of all three?
3. Are these areas commonly near mountain ranges, near oceans, or far away from both—or does it seem to be a mixture?
4. Are these areas near the equator or nearer to the North Pole or South Pole?
5. Next, identify at least 10 areas that have low average rainfall. Do steps 2, 3, and 4 with them.
6. What can you say about the effect altitude has on rainfall?
7. What effect do mountain ranges and oceans seem to have on rainfall?
8. What effect does latitude (distance from the equator) have on rainfall?

## *TEACHER INFORMATION*

Latitude determines which *wind belt* a region is located in and, to a large degree, whether the region will have warm, moist air creating rainy weather, or cool, dry air bringing dry weather. Rainfall is also affected by mountains, usually favoring the windward side of the mountain. As the air moves up the mountainside it is cooled and condensed and rainfall results. The leeward side of the mountain gets the air mass after much of the moisture has been condensed from the air. As winds blow inland from the ocean, the regions nearest the ocean get the most rainfall, when moisture condenses out of the ocean air blowing across the land.

# ACTIVITY 90:  How Is the Earth Like a Jigsaw Puzzle?

(Total or small-group activity)

## *MATERIALS NEEDED*

- Globe of the earth
- Soccer ball
- Tennis ball cut in half

## *PROCEDURE*

1. Look at the three objects on the table. They represent different models of what scientists think our earth is like.
2. The thin outer cover of the tennis ball represents our earth's crust, the part on which we live. The model would be more accurate if we filled the rest of the ball with very hot metal, but we won't do that.
3. Examine the soccer ball. Notice it is not just a smooth, round ball, but appears to be made of many pieces. In some ways, the crust of our earth is like the soccer ball; scientists believe it is not a single, solid piece or cover, but many pieces that fit together in different ways. This idea is called *plate tectonics.*
4. Now look at the globe of the earth. Pretend it is a big jigsaw puzzle. If you could move the continents around, could you find a way to make them fit together?
5. Most scientists believe that millions of years ago the continents were joined together in some way and have gradually drifted apart. They call this idea (theory) *continental drift.*

## *TEACHER INFORMATION*

Some students may be unable to visualize the shapes of the continents in such a way that they can put them together. It may be helpful to make outline maps (cutouts) of the major continents to assist them.

**CAUTION: Carefully puncture the tennis ball before cutting it.**

# ACTIVITY 91:  How Is the Earth Like Your Body?

(Total-group activity)

## *MATERIALS NEEDED*

- Pencil
- Lined paper
- Picture of the earth
- Picture of the moon

## *PROCEDURE*

1. Scientists often refer to our earth as a living planet. Unlike the moon, which is considered dead, the earth is constantly changing its surface, using energy from the sun to grow new life, repairing damage to itself and adjusting its surface in response to many stresses. Compare the pictures of the earth and the moon. Can you see how one might be called living and the other dead?
2. Your body works in much the same way. Its surface changes, it has mountains and valleys, it is covered by a thin crust (skin), and it uses energy from the sun to grow. It also has the ability to repair itself when it is injured.
3. With your teacher and others, discuss what it means to be alive and why our living earth is so important to us.

## *TEACHER INFORMATION*

This activity and Activity 90 are intended to provide the foundation for the more specific activities that follow. First are activities concerned with general major phenomena, such as mountain building through earthquakes, folding, faulting, volcanic activity, and water and glacial erosion. Other activities focus on collecting and testing rocks in the student's immediate environment.

# ACTIVITY 92: What Factors Affect Water Erosion?

## *MATERIALS NEEDED*

- Two identical erosion trays
- Sprinkler
- Two basins, such as plastic dish-pans
- Water

- Several books
- Soil
- Leaves, sticks, and small rocks
- Paper towels

## *PROCEDURE*

1. Put an equal amount of soil on the two erosion trays.
2. Spread several leaves, sticks, and small rocks over the top of the soil in one tray.
3. Tilt both trays at the same angle and place the basins below the trays as illustrated. Sprinkle one quart of water over each one. First predict which tray will lose the most soil.

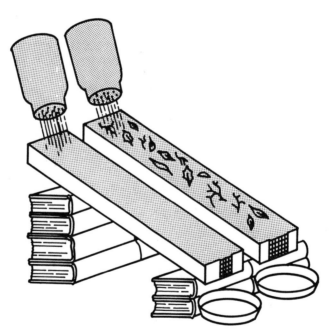

FIGURE 92-1. Erosion trays.

4. Use paper towels to filter out all the soil that was washed away in the quart of water. Was your prediction in step 3 correct?
5. Again place equal amounts of soil on the two trays. This time, leave the soil bare on each tray.

6.  Lower one tray slightly and raise the other slightly. Which do you think will lose the most soil during a "rainstorm?"
7.  Sprinkle one quart of water over each of the two trays and filter out the soil that is washed away. Was your prediction in step 6 correct?
8.  Compare the amount of soil washed away in step 7 with the amount washed away in step 3.
9.  What can you say about soil erosion in the mountains and factors that affect it?
10. Try to think of other ideas you could try to find out what might make soil erosion occur faster or more slowly.

## TEACHER INFORMATION

In this activity students will learn that erosion occurs faster on steeper slopes and that erosion is retarded by plant growth and debris.

The "erosion trays" could be as simple as two or three layers of cardboard. They could also be made from a sheet of aluminum or sheet metal. Old plastic dishpans could be used by cutting the sides down part way and cutting one end out. Cookie sheets can also be used.

For the sprinkler, a watering can designed for flowers will work well, or simply use a quart jar and punch several holes in the lid with a sharp instrument.

Let students devise additional erosion activities using the same equipment. For instance, they could get a small slab of sod from the edge of the lawn and test it for erosion. Try some of the loose soil with leaves, sticks, and rocks mixed in as well as lying on top of the soil. Compare sandy soil with clay soil.

# ACTIVITY 93: What Causes Earthquakes?

## *MATERIALS NEEDED*

- Several colors of clay

## *PROCEDURE*

1. Select one color of clay and make a flat sheet of it about 25 cm. long × 10 cm. wide × 5 mm. thick (10 in. × 4 in. × ¼ in.).
2. Make similar sheets of other colors of clay, varying the thickness somewhat.
3. Stack several strips of clay on top of each other.

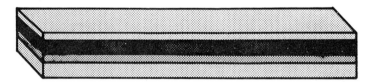

FIGURE 93-1. Stacked clay strips.

4. Put one hand on each end of the stack of clay and push toward the middle.
5. What happened?
6. If the layers of clay were layers of rock on the earth's surface, and they were forced together as you forced the clay in step 4, what would happen?

## *TEACHER INFORMATION*

Any soft plastic clay will work as clay for this activity. If sufficient clay is not available, carpet samples will do. You might think of other material that could be substituted, such as colored bath towels. Anything that can be layered and pushed together to show folding is adequate.

Although the layers of rock in the earth's surface are very hard and very heavy, heat and pressure under them are sometimes strong enough to cause them to shift, slide, and buckle. This results in earthquakes, and if it occurs in populated areas, much damage can occur.

You might want to let the layers of clay dry somewhat in order to better resemble the brittle rock layers as folding occurs, or wet the surface of each layer, so the layers are more likely to slide on each other as rock layers sometimes do.

If cracks are noted in the layers of clay, point out that these represent *joints*. Sometimes rock layers shift at joints. Cracks along which movement has occurred are called *faults*. If there is an earth fault reasonably nearby, a visit to it would make an excellent field trip. Students could construct a model of the earth layers from clay as they think the area of the fault might appear.

# ACTIVITY 94: How Can You Make a Volcano Replica?

## *MATERIALS NEEDED*

- Large pan
- Rubber tubing 50 cm. (20 in.) long
- Flour
- Salt

- Water
- Puffed rice
- Brown tempera paint
- Paintbrush
- Pencil

## *PROCEDURE*

1. Make at least two quarts of salt-flour paste in the pan.
2. In the same pan, form the salt-flour paste into a volcano-like cone, leaving a cone-shaped hole in the center (Figure 94-1).

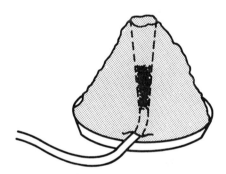

FIGURE 94-1. Volcano replica.

3. Use a pencil to form a small tunnel under one side of the volcano. Then insert the tube into the tunnel and bring it up in the center of the volcano so that the end of the tube comes up in the bottom of the cone. Seal the channel by pressing the paste around the tube.
4. When the model dries and hardens, paint it with brown tempera paint.
5. Pour some puffed rice into the cone.
6. Blow on the end of the tube, gently at first, then harder.
7. What happened? From the way your model works, tell what you can about real volcanoes.

## *TEACHER INFORMATION*

In this model, air pressure forces the cereal out of the vent, simulating an eruption. In real volcanoes, the pressure is created by heat, steam, and movements beneath the earth's surface. This experience should be followed by a discussion of the similarities and differences between the model and a real volcano. Volcanic eruptions form mountains. Some islands, such as the Hawaiian Islands, are the tops of such mountains formed in the ocean.

A more realistic model can be made by using ammonium dichromate (crystal form) for the erupting material (Figure 94-2). If you use this, certain changes should be made in the construction of the volcano. Instead of forming the inside cone, place a small tin can in the top and mold the clay around it. Omit the rubber tube and the puffed rice. You might want to make the volcano out of plaster of Paris instead of salt-flour clay. The ammonium dichromate is placed in the can and is to be lit with a match. You might need to add a bit of alcohol or lighter fluid to get it to light. **CAUTION: The operation of this volcano must be closely supervised and the volcano should be used outdoors. Have students stand back before the volcano is lit.** With proper supervision, this volcano is safe and provides a rather realistic impression of the volcanic eruption. Be sure to wash your hands thoroughly after this activity, as the ash produced during the eruption is poisonous, and the ammonium dichromate is more so. The volcano should be placed on newspapers, then, when finished, gathered up and thrown away.

FIGURE 94-2. Volcano replica made with ammonium dichromate.

If you have access to a compressed air source, even a portable air tank, you should consider another style of volcano model that is safe, realistic, and easy to construct. Insert a rubber tube through the bottom of a cardboard box at the center and attach it with tape (the opening of the tube should be very near the bottom of the box). The box should be at least 30 cm. (12 in.) square. Put a layer of sand in the box, at least 10 cm. (4 in.) deep. Turn on the air slowly at first, then increase the pressure. Too much air pressure will blow sand farther than you probably want it. A "volcanic" cone will form in a natural way, as the sand is blown up and falls back to the surface (Figure 94-3).

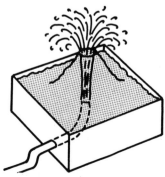

FIGURE 94-3. Volcano replica made with compressed air.

# ACTIVITY 95: How Is Snow Compacted into Ice to Form Glaciers?

## MATERIALS NEEDED

- Tall, narrow jar with lid
- Rocks or other weights that can fit into jar
- Scissors
- Cardboard
- Masking tape
- Fresh marshmallows
- Pencil

## PROCEDURE

1. Fill the jar with marshmallows, loosely packed.
2. Cut a cardboard circle to fit inside the jar without rubbing the sides.
3. Place the rocks, or other weights, on top of the cardboard circle.
4. Stick a strip of masking tape to the side of the jar from top to bottom.
5. Make a pencil mark on the masking tape at the level of the cardboard.
6. Put the lid on the jar and set the jar in a safe place.
7. Twice each day for four days, check the jar and make a pencil mark on the jar at the level of the cardboard.
8. At the end of four days, discuss your observations with others. Tell how you think this is like the forming of a glacier.

## TEACHER INFORMATION

As snow accumulates and remains for long periods of time, the weight of the snow compacts the lower layers into ice. If conditions are such that the accumulation continues season after season, glaciers are formed. In this activity, the compacting action is demonstrated with marshmallows. The weights substitute for upper layers of heavy snow. The lid is used to keep the marshmallows from drying out so the compacting action can continue for a longer period of time.

# ACTIVITY 96:  In What Order Do Materials Settle in Water?

## MATERIALS NEEDED

- 1-quart or larger glass jar with lid
- Gravel (rocks of varied sizes)
- Water
- Soil
- Sand

## PROCEDURE

1. Add equal amounts of the soil, gravel, and sand until the jar is about one-third full.
2. Add enough water so that the jar is almost full.
3. Place the lid on the jar and shake it carefully to thoroughly stir the mixture.
4. Which of the materials inside the jar do you think will settle to the bottom? Which will be on top?
5. Stop shaking the jar and let it stand until all materials are settled and the water is somewhat clear.
6. Examine the materials in the jar and record the order in which they settle to the bottom.
7. How accurate were your predictions?
8. Shake the mixture again and find out if the materials settle in the same order as the first time.
9. Try to explain why the materials settled out of the water in the order that they did. Do you think materials would settle in the same order at the bottom of the sea? What factors do you think would control the rate at which sediment settles to the ocean floor?

## TEACHER INFORMATION

If pieces of seashells or snail shells are available, add them to the materials in the bottle at step 1. Students will find that sediment will be rather consistently in order, with the largest rocks settling to the bottom and the fine sand and silt at the top. Some of the factors students should consider in step 9 are: size of the particle, density of the particle, shape of the particle, and water currents.

# ACTIVITY 97:  How Are Rocks Classified?

## *MATERIALS NEEDED*

- A collection of rocks
- Encyclopedia
- Other reference books as available.

## *PROCEDURE*

1. What colors are the rocks in this collection?
2. Classify (sort) the rocks by putting them into groups according to their color.
3. Do the rocks have different textures? Are some rough, some smooth, some shiny, and some dull? If so, classify them again according to their texture.
4. As you lift the rocks, do they all seem to have about the same density? In other words, do they seem to be about the same weight relative to their size? If not, classify them again according to density.
5. Look at the rocks carefully and see if you can think of any other characteristics you could use to classify them. If you think of any, sort the rocks again by those characteristics.
6. Look up "Rocks" in the encyclopedia or other reference books and find out what characteristics geologists use to classify rocks. See if you can tell what some of the rocks in this group are called.

## *TEACHER INFORMATION*

If some students have rock collections, this would be an excellent time to bring them to share with the class. These students are likely to have some degree of experience and expertise in collecting and identifying rocks that they can share with the group. In addition, a parent or brother or sister might be a "rockhound" and available as a resource person. Consider also the possibility of inviting a local geologist, forester, or manager of a rock shop.

As students learn to classify a few rocks, either by standard techniques or from ideas devised by the class, a field trip to a nearby canyon could provide a meaningful and lasting learning experience.

Don't overlook the value of the creative classification experience in the above activity. Resource people and reference books should come on the scene *after* students have had this opportunity to examine several rocks, describe them, identify likenesses and differences, and reason out in their minds some logical classifying characteristics.

The following activities will get students involved in testing for some of the characteristics used by experts in classifying rocks.

# ACTIVITY 98: How Do Rocks Compare in Hardness?

(Teacher-supervised activity)

## *MATERIALS NEEDED*

- Variety of rocks
- Dull knife, piece of glass, and other "scratchers"

## *PROCEDURE*

1. Select two rocks from the collection.
2. Try to scratch one with the other.
3. Which would you say is harder—the one that will scratch or the one that can be scratched?
4. Keep the harder of the two rocks and set the other aside.
5. Select another rock and use the same scratch test to compare it with the first one you kept.
6. Again keep the harder of the two rocks and set the other one aside.
7. Repeat the procedure until you have identified the hardest rock in the collection.
8. Now compare the other rocks and find the second hardest one. Put it next to the hardest.
9. Continue this process until you have all the rocks lined up in order of hardness.
10. Use the scratch test to compare other objects with rocks. Some things you might try are your fingernail, a knife blade, and a piece of glass. Be extremely careful with these sharp objects.
11. Try to find other rocks that are harder or softer than any you have in this collection.

## *TEACHER INFORMATION*

The label "rock" is often used rather loosely to mean either rock or mineral. Actually, rocks are made of minerals. Minerals have physical properties and chemical composition that either are fixed or vary within a limited range. A rock is often an aggregate of minerals.

Minerals are scaled in hardness in a range of 1 to 10, with 1 being very soft and 10 very hard. A common method of determining hardness is the "scratch test." Fingernails have a hardness of about 2.5, so if a rock will scratch the fingernail, the rock has a hardness greater than 2.5. If it will not scratch the fingernail, or if it can be scratched by the fingernail, the rock has a hardness less than 2.5. A penny has a hardness of three, so if a rock scratches the penny, it has a hardness greater than three. Other common materials that can be used in the scratch test are steel knife blades (hardness about 5.5), glass (hardness about 5.5 to 6.0), and other rocks.

The Mohs' hardness scale is helpful in comparing hardness of rocks. It uses the following minerals, representing hardnesses of 1 to 10:

1. talc
2. gypsum
3. calcite
4. fluorite
5. apatite
6. orthoclase feldspar
7. quartz
8. topaz
9. corundum
10. diamond

*NOTE:* In step 10 above, you will need to judge whether students are to use knife blades and glass in their comparisons. Other objects can be tested to see where they lie in the range of hardness.

# ACTIVITY 99: What Color Streak Does a Rock Make?

## *MATERIALS NEEDED*

- Collection of rocks
- Porcelain
- Sheets of paper in various colors
- Colored pencils

## *PROCEDURE*

1. Select one of the rocks from the collection.
2. Try to make a streak on the porcelain with the rock.
3. Does it make a streak? If so, what color streak does it make?
4. Try to make a streak with each of the other rocks in the collection.
5. Does the color of the streak usually match the color of the rock that made it?
6. Put the rocks in groups according to the color of the streak.
7. Will any of your rocks write on paper? Try it. Draw a picture if you'd like. Try different colors of paper as well as different types of rocks.

## *TEACHER INFORMATION*

One of the common tests made in classifying rocks is the *streak test*. A porcelain plate, called a *streak plate*, is used. The rock is rubbed on the streak plate to see what color dust it makes. A broken piece of porcelain dish or white porcelain tile will suffice as the streak plate.

**(CAUTION: If you use a broken piece of porcelain as the streak plate, close supervision is needed to assure safety.)** The color of the streak is frequently different from the color of the rock that made it.

If the rock collection includes talc, anthracite (coal), or gypsum, students should be able to write on paper with them.

# ACTIVITY 100:   How Do Rocks React to Vinegar?

## *MATERIALS NEEDED*

- Collection of rocks
- One plastic cup for each rock
- Vinegar
- Chalk

## *PROCEDURE*

1. Put a very small sample of each rock in a separate cup. Put a small piece of chalk in a cup as one of the rock samples.
2. Pour a small amount of vinegar on each sample.
3. What happened?
4. Group the rocks according to the way they responded to the vinegar.

## *TEACHER INFORMATION*

This test is called the *acid test* and is normally performed with dilute hydrochloric acid (HC1). Vinegar is a weak acid and works satisfactorily.

The acid test is used to identify rocks that contain calcium carbonate. Any such rock will fizz when vinegar (or dilute HC1) is applied. Limestone, marble, calcite, and chalk are made of calcium carbonate and will fizz in the presence of vinegar.

# ACTIVITY 101:  Which Rocks Are Attracted by a Magnet?

## *MATERIALS NEEDED*

- Collection of rocks
- Magnet

## *PROCEDURE*

1. Select one of the rocks and touch it with the magnet.
2. Is this rock attracted by the magnet?
3. Test each rock in the collection to see if any seem to contain magnetic material.
4. Make two groups of rocks—those that are attracted by the magnet, and those that are not.

## *TEACHER INFORMATION*

Try to include at least one rock that contains iron, such as galena, in the collection of rocks used for this activity. If no rocks that are attracted by a magnet are available, this activity should be omitted.

If you have, or can acquire, a piece of magnetite (lodestone) it would make an excellent addition to the collection for this exercise. Magnetite is nature's magnet. After the activity is completed as written, have students suspend the magnetite from a string and see how it responds to the magnet. It will be attracted or repelled, depending on its position, the same as any magnet behaves in the presence of another magnet.

(For more information on magnetism, see Section 7 in Book 2: Physical Sciences of the *Library*.)

# ACTIVITY 102: Which Rocks Conduct Electricity?

## *MATERIALS NEEDED*

- Collection of rocks
- Dry cell battery
- Small light socket with flash-light bulb
- Two pieces of insulated wire about 20 cm. (8 in.) long

- One piece of insulated wire about 5 cm. (2 in.) long
- Small bolt or nail

## *PROCEDURE*

1. Connect the bulb to the battery with the pieces of wire, as illustrated in Figure 102-1, to be sure the battery and bulb are working properly. Be sure you can light the bulb before going on to the next step.

FIGURE 102-1. Flashlight cell, bulb, and wires.

2. Use both wires and connect the system again, this time with the bolt held between the two wires (Figure 102-2). Be sure you can light the bulb this way before you continue. The bolt is a good conductor of electricity.

FIGURE 102-2. Same as Figure 102-1, but with a bolt in the circuit.

3. Remove the bolt and put one of the rocks in its place. Does the bulb light? If so, the rock is a conductor of electricity.
4. Put the rocks in two groups—those that are conductors of electricity and those that are nonconductors. (If the bulb lights, the rock is a conductor.)

## TEACHER INFORMATION

Some rocks conduct electricity (such as those containing significant amounts of copper, zinc, or iron). This is one of the characteristics scientists use in classifying and identifying rocks.

# ACTIVITY 103: How Can Rocks Be Dissolved in Water?

## *MATERIALS NEEDED*

- Small pieces of limestone
- Corrugated cardboard
- Plastic wrap or large plastic bag
- Piece of clear glass
- Rainwater
- Vinegar

## *PROCEDURE*

1. Make a long trough of the corrugated cardboard and line it with plastic.
2. Prop one end of the trough so that it tilts slightly.
3. If the limestone is not in small pieces, break it up with a hammer or with another rock.
4. Wash the pieces of limestone with clean rainwater and spread them along the trough.
5. Add clean rainwater very slowly, drop by drop, at the top of the trough.
6. Clean the clear glass well and place it under the lower end of the trough to catch several drops of water that have soaked through the limestone.

FIGURE 103-1. Trough lined with plastic, pieces of limestone, and glass.

7. Let the water evaporate from the glass.
8. Examine the dry glass. What do you see? Is it still perfectly clean? If not, what is on it?
9. What if this same process occurs with mountains of limestone and millions of gallons of rainwater? What happens? What has this to do with the formation of limestone caverns?
10. Repeat the activity, using vinegar in the place of rainwater at step 5. If you notice any difference in the amount of material deposited on the glass, try to explain why.

## *TEACHER INFORMATION*

Water containing weak acids will actually dissolve limestone, as is witnessed by the formation of many caves and caverns, both large and small. Once caverns have been formed, water keeps dripping into them and the rock material comes out of solution forming stalagmites and stalactites.

The dissolving process is speeded up as the acid content increases. This is demonstrated by the use of vinegar. The acid involved is mostly carbonic acid, formed when water dissolves carbon dioxide. Other acids are contained in some air pollutants and washed out of the air by rain. This is called *acid rain*, and it can be harmful to plant and animal life and water supplies.

# ACTIVITY 104: How Do Crystals Form?

(Teacher-supervised activity)

## MATERIALS NEEDED

- Heat source
- Metal saucepan
- 3 ounces of powdered alum
- String
- Fruit jar

- Filter paper or cotton cloth
- Water
- Magnifying glass
- Pencil
- Small rock or other weight

## PROCEDURE

1. Measure one quart of water and pour it into the saucepan.
2. Heat to boiling point.
3. Sprinkle the alum into the water and stir.
4. Pour the hot water into the fruit jar, straining it with the filter or cloth.
5. Tie a piece of string to a pencil. Tie a small rock (or other small weight) to the other end of the string. Lay the pencil across the top of the jar, and let the string hang down into the water.

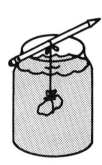

FIGURE 104-1. String hanging into water from a pencil.

6. Let the solution stand for one full day, occasionally examining it to see what happens.
7. What formed in the jar? Look at it carefully.
8. Carefully remove the string from the jar and examine it with a magynifying glass. What do you see? Describe the shapes.

## TEACHER INFORMATION

As the solution cools, alum crystals will form in the jar and on the string. Careful examination with a magnifying glass should reveal the crystals to be diamond-shaped.

After students have completed this activity, have them repeat it, using table salt instead of alum. Salt crystals will form from a saturated salt solution and the crystals will be cube-shaped. Students should discover this difference as they examine and compare. Then try the same activity with sugar. Students should begin to realize that each substance produces its own unique crystal.

# ACTIVITY 105: What Type of Crystals Do Rocks Have?

## *MATERIALS NEEDED*

- Collection of rocks
- Hand lens

## *PROCEDURE*

1. Examine each rock with the hand lens.
2. Can you see any crystal structure?
3. Are the crystals lined up or are they arranged randomly?
4. Do the crystals seem to be somewhat interlocking (melted together) or do they appear to be glued together by a cementing material?
5. Put the rocks in groups according to your findings.

## *TEACHER INFORMATION*

Igneous and metamorphic rocks have undergone intense heat in their formation and the crystals are interlocking, or melted together by nature, with materials that settled to the bottom of a body of water where the rock was formed. Beautiful arrangements of quartz crystals are found in the centers of hollow rocks called geodes. Try to include at least one geode in the collection used.

# ACTIVITY 106:  What Is Conglomerate Rock?

## *MATERIALS NEEDED*

- Dry cement
- Dry sand
- Variety of rocks
- Plastic-lined shoe box

- Water
- Stick
- Magnifying glass

## *PROCEDURE*

1. Put one cup of dry cement, one cup of dry sand, and one cup of cold water into the plastic-lined shoe box and stir with the stick. Be sure to mix it thoroughly.
2. Stir your rocks into the mixture.
3. Let the mixture stand for two or three days.
4. What happened to the mixture?
5. Take your mixture out of the shoe box and remove the plastic.
6. Use the magnifying glass to examine your mixture. Can you see some of the rocks you put in it? Can you see the sand?

## *TEACHER INFORMATION*

A conglomerate rock is made of various smaller rocks that have become cemented together by nature, quite like the block of concrete students make in the above activity. For obvious reasons, the rocks used for this activity should not be from a rock collection that someone wants to keep.

A small conglomerate rock formed by nature would be an excellent visual aid to accompany this activity. A field trip to an area where students can find conglomerate rocks in nature makes an excellent learning activity. Students could also examine sidewalks, concrete walls, and bricks to compare and find evidence of the "conglomerate."

# ACTIVITY 107: How Do You Start a Rock Collection?

## MATERIALS NEEDED

- Hammer and chisel
- Canvas bag (or other strong bag)
- At least three egg cartons
- Newspapers
- Marker

## PROCEDURE

1. Take your hammer, chisel, and bag and gather a few rocks to begin your rock collection. Around the school yard, at home, or on the way to school are good places to look. Try to find rocks of different colors and textures, and with other differences that you can see or feel.
2. It will probably be necessary to break up some of the rocks in order to get the right size specimen, or just to allow a better view of what the rock really looks like. When you break a rock, first put it in newspapers, a bag, or other covering to trap the flying pieces to avoid injury.
3. Sort your rocks into three main categories, as follows:
    a. *Sedimentary:* Have a layered appearance. Usually feel gritty and break easily.
    b. *Igneous:* Often crystalline appearance, never in layers.
    c. *Metamorphic:* Very hard, appear more crystalline than igneous rocks. Crystals of each mineral are lined up in bands or layers.
4. Label one egg carton "Sedimentary," one "Igneous," and one "Metamorphic," and put your rocks into the compartments of the appropriate egg carton.

## TEACHER INFORMATION

To add to an established rock collection, one might need to visit distant or hard-to-get-to locations, but the collection can be started anywhere. A stone quarry or area that has been excavated is an excellent location, but some very interesting rocks can often be collected around the yard at home, at school, or at the side of a road. Hillsides provide excellent prospects, as do stream beds. If rocks for student collection are not available in your area, try to find another source. For instance, students could write letters to friends and relatives in other parts of the country and ask for some small samples of rock common to their areas.

Students should be encouraged to collect rock specimens that are neither too large nor too small. The egg carton suggested for classification and storage helps in keeping size under control.

As students begin their rock collections, explain that it is very important to keep information such as collection location, date, collector, and rock type. An easy way to do this is to put a number on each rock, then write the information with that number in a notebook.

# ACTIVITY 108: What Other Classifications of Rocks Are There?

## MATERIALS NEEDED

- Rock collections in egg cartons from Activity 107
- Vinegar
- Masking tape
- Marker
- Porcelain or piece of white tile
- Rock identification charts and books
- Paper
- Pencil

## PROCEDURE

1. Use the masking tape and marker to put a number on each rock in the igneous collection.
2. List the numbers of the igneous rocks down the left side of your paper. Leave space at the right for recording information about the rocks.
3. Do the "scratch test" (see Activity 98) on each of the numbered rocks and record the rating on the paper.
4. Do the "streak test" (see Activity 99) on each of the numbered rocks and record the result on the paper.
5. Do the "acid test" (see Activity 100) on each of the numbered rocks and record the reaction on the paper.
6. Use rock and mineral identification charts in various references and decide what you think each rock is. Record your findings on the paper.
7. Now follow these same steps with your sedimentary collection and your metamorphic collection.

## TEACHER INFORMATION

Before beginning this activity, students should have already tried each of the tests (scratch, acid, and streak) in the activities referred to above. They should also have collected a variety of rocks and sorted them into the three major categories, using egg cartons as described in Activity 107.

Having completed these preliminary activities, students should be prepared to make a serious effort to further classify the rocks in their collection. Encylopedias and field manuals on rocks are excellent sources for identification charts.

# ACTIVITY 109: How Can You Make a Permanent Shell Imprint?

## *MATERIALS NEEDED*

- Seashell
- Pie tin
- Petroleum jelly
- Plaster of Paris
- Water
- Paper towels
- Newspapers

## *PROCEDURE*

1. Coat the bottom and sides of the pie tie tin with a thin layer of petroleum jelly so the plaster will release easily..
2. Coat your shell with a thin layer of petroleum jelly.
3. Lay your shell in the bottom of the pie tin. Place it with the rounded side up (Figure 109-1).

FIGURE 109-1. Shell, rounded side up, in pan.

4. Mix plaster with water according to the instructions on the package. Prepare sufficient plaster to make a layer in the pan about 15 mm. (at least ½ in.).
5. Pour the plaster carefully over the shell and let it harden (leave it at least one hour).
6. Turn the pie tin upside down on a table covered with newspaper and tap it lightly. The plaster cast with shell should fall out onto the table.
7. Remove the shell but handle the plaster cast very carefully. The plaster will be quite soft until it has had at least a day to cure (harden).
8. After at least one day of curing time, carefully wipe the excess petroleum jelly off the plaster cast with a paper towel. Then wash the rest off lightly with warm water.
9. You now have an imprint of the shell in plaster much like those often found in limestone and other sedimentary rock (Figure 109-2). When found in rock, this imprint is called a fossil because it is evidence of an ancient animal.

FIGURE 109-2. Shell imprint in plaster.

## TEACHER INFORMATION

Plaster of Paris can be obtained at a local builders supply store or hobby shop. It is easy to work with, and if students follow the directions, the project should be successful. As the plaster cures, it will become quite warm, then will cool. It should be allowed to cool completely before being removed from the mold (pie tin).

If you have an area nearby where fossils can be found, that would be an excellent field trip. Otherwise, perhaps a few fossil samples could be borrowed from a friend or purchased from a science supply house. The experience of making a "fossil" will make a more lasting impression on the minds of students if they can see just how similar their "fossil" is to the real fossil formed by nature.

The imprint resulting from the above activity is a negative imprint. If a positive image is desired, spread a thin layer of petroleum jelly on the entire surface of the plaster cast, wrap and tie a piece of cardboard around it to provide sideboards to hold plaster, and pour another layer of plaster on top of the first. After it has cured, remove the cardboard, separate the two pieces of plaster with a knife blade, and presto—you have both a positive and negative of the shell. Clean up the petroleum jelly after the plaster has cured thoroughly, as indicated above.

An imprint of a leaf can be made following the same steps.

# ACTIVITY 110: How Can You Measure the Density of a Rock?

(Enrichment activity or for older students)

## *MATERIALS NEEDED*

- Variety of small rocks
- Gram balance
- Beaker or soup can
- Small tray or pan
- Water
- Paper
- Pencil

## *PROCEDURE*

1.  Select a rock. It must fit inside your beaker.
2.  Weigh your rock on the gram balance and record the weight.
3.  Determine the weight of a volume of water equal to the volume of your rock by following these steps:
    a.  Place the tray on the balance. Weigh the tray and record its weight. Then place the beaker on the tray.
    b.  Pour as much water into the beaker as you can get in it without overflowing water into the tray. If any water spills into the tray, it must be cleaned up.
    c.  Carefully put your rock into the beaker of water. The water that is displaced by the rock will spill into the tray. It will have exactly the same volume as the rock.
    d.  Carefully remove the beaker without spilling any more water.
    e.  Weigh the tray containing the water and subtract the weight of the empty tray to obtain the weight of the water that was displaced by the rock.
4.  Divide the weight of the rock by the weight of the water it displaced.
5.  What is the result? This number represents the specific gravity of the rock.
6.  Follow the same procedure with rocks of other types and compare the specific gravity of the rocks.

## *TEACHER INFORMATION*

*Specific gravity* is a number expressing the ratio between the weight of an object and the weight of an equal volume of water at four degrees celsius. If a rock weighs twice as much as an equal volume of water, its specific gravity is 2. If it weighs three times as much as an equal volume of water, its specific gravity is 3, and so on. Most common minerals have a specific gravity of about 2.5–3.0. Those outside these limits feel noticeably light or noticeably heavy.

If a gram balance is not available, try a postage scale or other sensitive scale.

# ACTIVITY 111: What Can You Learn from a Square Meter of Soil?

## *MATERIALS NEEDED*

- Meter stick or measuring tape
- Small shovel
- Magnifying glass
- Ball of string
- Tongue depressors
- Paper and pencil
- Encyclopedias and other resources

## *PROCEDURE*

1. Measure off one square meter (or one square yard) of soil.
2. Mark your plot of ground by outlining it with string, anchoring your string at the corners with tongue depressors.
3. Select a place to begin, perhaps at one corner.
4. Write down all the things you can find within your square meter (yard), including each type of grass, weed, insect, rock, and so forth. Describe or draw the different types of plant and animal life.
5. Dig into the soil. Add to your list anything else you find, such as worms, more insects, roots, or rocks.
6. Pick up a handful of soil. Feel it and describe it on your paper. Is it hard, soft, spongy, moist, or dry? Does it pack into a ball when you squeeze it, or does it remain loose? Is it sandy?
7. Now examine your plants, insects, rocks, and soil with the magnifying glass and see how much additional information you can write down— things you could not see or did not notice without the magnifying glass.
8. Try to find out the names of some of the plants, animals, and rocks on your list. Use encyclopedias, field manuals, or resource people you think might know.

## *TEACHER INFORMATION*

We so often look without seeing. Students will be amazed at how much they learn from a tiny plot of ground—perhaps an area they have walked across, or near to, many times. Encourage students, especially those who show high interest in this activity, to select another plot and repeat the steps above. Suggest that the second plot be some distance from the first—at home, for instance. Compare information from the two. If interest continues, this activity could be repeated several times, with new information and new insights gained each time.

This could also provide an excellent opportunity to develop a study of how soil is formed from rocks and other materials.

# ACTIVITY 112:  How Is Soil Made?

## *MATERIALS NEEDED*

- Rocks
- Sand
- Magnifying glass

- Leaves
- Soil
- Dishpan or bucket

## *PROCEDURE*

1. Examine the rocks and sand with the magnifying glass.
2. How are the rocks and sand alike? How are they different?
3. Each grain of sand was once a part of a rock and was broken off by natural forces. As the sand is ground finer and finer and mixed with organic material, such as decaying plant material, soil is formed. This process take a long time for nature to perform.
4. Put a thick layer of sand in the pan or bucket.
5. Break up some leaves, or other plant material, into tiny pieces. You could even grind this material up between two rocks.
6. Mix the fine plant material into the sand. Use about the same amount of this material as sand.
7. Compare your mixture with the soil. What likenesses do you observe? What differences?
8. If you can, set your mixture and soil aside for several weeks. Then compare them again.

## *TEACHER INFORMATION*

Soil begins to form when rocks and similar materials on or near the earth's surface are broken down by environmental forces. The substance that results from this action is called *parent material*. Parent material is broken down into mineral particles through a process called *weathering*. There are two kinds of weathering: *physical disintegration* (caused by such forces as ice and rain) and *chemical decomposition* (such as when water dissolves certain minerals in a rock).Through the centuries, organic material mixes with the parent material and the resultant matter resembles the parent material less and less.

Various environmental factors affect soil formation, including climate, land surface features, plants and animals present, kinds of parent material, and time. The mineral content of parent material helps determine the kinds of plants that grow in the soil.

Just as soil is constantly being formed, it is also constantly being destroyed by erosive forces such as wind and water.

Although this activity will not produce real soil, it will result in a soil-like material and will provide a glimpse of nature's soil-making process. If circum-

stances will allow, let the mixture stand for a period of several weeks or months. Leaves break down quite rapidly and the substance will appear more like soil than when first mixed.

Consider having students crush their own rocks by using other rocks or hammers. If this is done, however, be sure adequate protection from flying chips is provided, especially for the eyes. Also be cautious of possible injury to fingers in the pounding process. Sand can similarly be ground into powder, resulting in a more soil-like mixture.

Other organic matter can be substituted for the leaves, or added to them.

*Section 6*

---

# *ECOLOGY*

# TO THE TEACHER

Ecology is both *inter*disciplinary and *intra*disciplinary. It is *inter*disciplinary because it involves content from the biological, physical, and earth sciences, plus all areas of the social sciences. It is *intra*disciplinary because the ecologist attempts to use information from many sources to produce a unique field.

Many of the ecological problems we read about, see on TV, or hear on the radio are global in nature. Some are highly sensitive and fall in the political realm. National and international relations often deteriorate over ecologically based issues. This section does not attempt to deal with moral, economic, or political issues. It deals with some basics of the science of ecology and attempts to help students realize their place, as individuals, in the ecological system.

The first portion of the area deals in very simple ways with nature's balance, food cycles, and food webs. The chemical cycles of soil, water, and air are alluded to but not introduced formally. If you care to pursue these in greater depth, your library can provide ample resources.

People are introduced into an ecological system in the second section. From that point, liberties are taken with the term *ecosystem* to generalize it to apply to the student and his or her interaction with the immediate environment.

For the remainder of the section, human interaction with the *immediate* environment becomes the focal point. Conservation, cooperation, and individual responsibility are emphasized. You may be tempted as many are, to become preachy at this point; however, the effectiveness will be greatly increased if students are helped to discover these ideas on their own.

Throughout the book, discovery/inquiry and verbal responses have been emphasized. In this section, pictures, charts, and written work should be saved for a final, culminating activity.

At the end of several activities, a specific film or VCR is recommended. Most are from the Walt Disney Studios. Other films should be added or substituted when appropriate. Teachers of young children should be aware that some of the films show predators killing prey and portray life and death as they occur in a true ecosystem. Be sure to order the films well in advance and preview them.

Try to include as much art, music, poetry, and aesthetic experience as you can. Opportunities for enrichment are almost limitless.

# ACTIVITY 113: Where Can We Begin?

(Introductory teacher demonstration)

## *MATERIALS NEEDED*

- Classroom wastebasket
- Tape recorder
- 90-minute blank recording tape

- Large photograph of earth taken by astronauts as they stood on the moon.

## *TEACHER INFORMATION*

This activity is suggested as a way to interest children in ecology as it directly affects their lives. It has proven successful in many classrooms. If you feel it is not appropriate for your group, begin with Activity 114.

1. Make a tape recording by someone with a deep, sonorous voice. This recording should have a few minutes of blank tape at the beginning. Place it in a battery-operated tape recorder, buried (but protected) under litter in your classroom wastebasket. Turn it on just before school begins or after lunch.

2. After the few minutes of blank tape, the wastebasket will say some of the following (adapt the taped message to fit your own situation):

    a. Call out several times (ask to be put on the table).

    b. Call attention to the kinds of things people are throwing away.

    c. Point out the condition of the classroom.

    d. Talk about hearing complaints from the garbage can where all school refuse is dumped; also the waste cans in the lunch room.

    e. Call the attention of the class to the photo of the earth taken by astronauts as they stood on the moon. Point out that this is all we have—this fragile globe on which we live; when it's gone, what do we do?

    f. Ask the students if they have ever heard of a food chain or ecosystem. Remind them that they are supposed to be consumers, not wasters. Consumers make contributions. Offer to tell them some ways they can help.

    g. Say, "Ms. or Mr. (teacher's name), tell everyone about the bulletin board you have on the wall."

At this point (if you choose to use a "talking wastebasket") move to the bulletin board in Activity 114.

# ACTIVITY 114: What Is a Simple Plant-Animal Community?

## *MATERIALS NEEDED*

- 24″ × 36″ labeled poster of Figure 114-1
- 8½″ × 11″ unlabeled copy of Figure 114-1 for each student
- Crayons
- Pencils

## *PROCEDURE*

1. Compare your picture with the one on the bulletin board. This is a basic grassland community. It has six important elements. As your teacher explains the function of each, color it on your paper.
2. Energy from the sun in the form of heat and light is the very first ingredient. Without it, nothing else could happen. Label and color the sun.
3. Air must be present before life can exist. Since air is colorless, write "air" on a blank spot somewhere below the sun.
4. Moisture in some form must also be present. How do you think this grassland is getting moisture? Label and show it in some way on your picture.
5. Good soil is necessary for grassy or woody plants. Soil has dead leaves and sticks *(humus)* in it. There are also small animals called *scavengers* such as worms, bugs, and beetles. Scavengers feed on dead plant and animal materials in the soil and break it down into smaller parts. Tiny bacteria and fungi called *decomposers* further break down materials into minerals that plants need to grow. Color and label the humus, scavengers, and decomposers.
6. Plants of many kinds grow above the ground. They all depend on energy from the sun, air, moisture, and rich soil. In turn, they remove carbon dioxide from, and release oxygen into the air. They give off moisture. Most plants use energy from the sun combined with moisture and rich soil to produce food. They are the *primary producers* of food on the earth. Without them, other forms of life could not exist. Color the plants and flowers in your picture.
7. Your grassland community is now working. Save it for use later on.

## *TEACHER INFORMATION*

In the study of this portion of ecology we will consider groups or types of living and nonliving things interacting with each other as *communities*. When we add animals as primary and secondary consumers, we will then have an *ecosystem*.

Ecosystems can be as simple as a balanced aquarium in a classroom or as complex as an entire region, or country, or the world. Our studies will be confined to small communities and ecosystems to provide simple examples with which the students can relate.

As people are introduced into ecosystems, students will begin to understand how complex the problems can become.

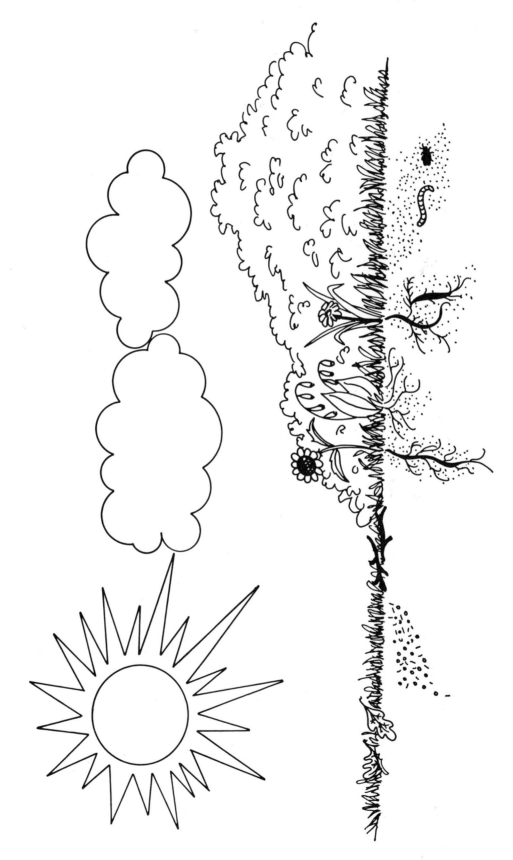

FIGURE 114-1. Profile of grassland community.

# ACTIVITY 115:  What Is a Pond Community?

## *MATERIALS NEEDED*

- Student copy of grassland picture from Activity 114
- 8½" × 11" unlabeled copy of Figure 115-1 for each student

- Crayons
- Pencil

## *PROCEDURE*

1. Compare the picture you made of the grassland community and the new picture you have.
2. This is a picture of a pond community. It is sometimes called an ecosystem. Label and color all the nonliving elements as you did in your last picture. If there are any new nonliving things, label and color them.
3. Use your picture from the last activity to label as many other similar things (grasses, scavengers, decomposers) as you can.
4. What new things are unlabeled and uncolored?
5. The animals in the picture do not produce food; they consume it. They are called *consumers*.
6. Animals that feed on primary producers (plants, grasses, and algae) are called *primary consumers*. Animals that usually feed on other animals are called *secondary consumers*.
7. In your picture, the small animals (shrimp, water flea, and snail) are primary consumers feeding on plants and algae. Label and color them.
8. The fish and frog are secondary consumers in this instance, since they feed on small primary consumers. Label and color them.
9. The snake is a higher-level secondary consumer who may eat either the frog or the fish. Label and color it.
10. The bird (in this case a blue heron) is an even higher level of secondary consumer because it may eat the fish, frog, or snake. Label and color it.
11. Whether an animal is a primary or secondary consumer depends on what it eats, not on its size. The elephant is a primary consumer. A ladybug beetle is a secondary consumer.
12. Turn your paper over and draw a picture of the plants and animals in your classroom aquarium. Can you find both producers and consumers?

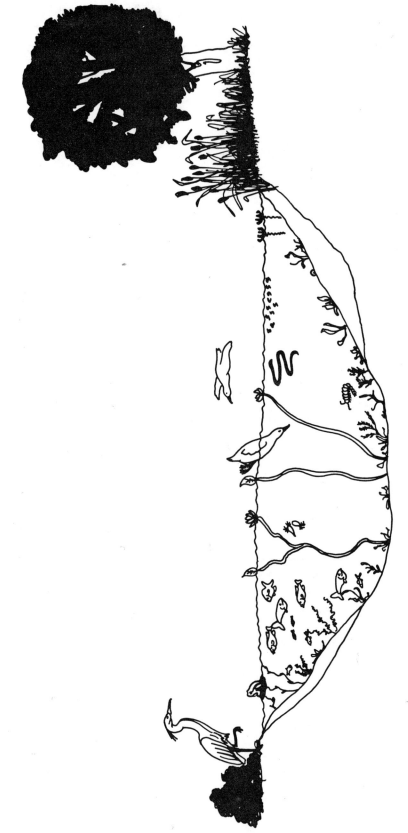

FIGURE 115-1. Pond ecosystem.

## TEACHER INFORMATION

If you do not have a freshwater aquarium or a good terrarium—and have not developed one earlier in the year—this would be an excellent time. As students learn more about ecosystems, they will be able to have first-hand experience with a simple model.

As we add primary and secondary consumers to the model, the system becomes far more complex. Up to this point, the terms *herbivore* (plant eater), *carnivore* (animal eater), and *omnivore* (eats both plants and animals) have not been introduced. They are not necessary to the understanding of ecosytems.

# ACTIVITY 116: What Is a Simple Ecosystem?

## *MATERIALS NEEDED*

- Picture of grassland community developed in Activity 115
- Pencil
- Crayons
- Pictures of animals shown in Figures 116-1, 116-2, and 116-3

## *PROCEDURE*

1. Figures 116-1 and 116-2 show animals that might live in a grassland community. Some are primary consumers and some are secondary consumers. Draw the ground animals on your picture of a grassland community. Color them.
2. Some birds are primary consumers. They eat berries and seeds. Others are secondary consumers who prey on primary consumers. Can you tell which is which? HINT: Look at their beaks and claws.
3. Now that we have added consumers, our grassland ecosystem is complete. However, we have two new kinds of animals. The smaller bird is a *migratory* animal who joins the ecosystem for a period of time when certain seeds or berries are ripe and then moves on to another location. On your picture of a grassland community, draw a migratory bird. Color it.
4. The second, larger bird is a *predator*. It preys on smaller animals. Notice its large, powerful claws and sharp beak. Some *predators* are migratory but many are permanent residents, depending on the food supply. Draw the *predator* on your picture of a grassland community. Color it.
5. Figure 116-3 shows some larger animals that might be found in a grassland community. Two are primary consumers. One is a predator, or secondary consumer. If you know what they eat, you can tell them apart. On your grassland community draw the new animals. Color them.
6. Now that you have developed both a pond and a grassland ecosytem, can you think of the reason why plants and animals live together and are dependent on each other?

## *TEACHER INFORMATION*

As consumers and migratory animals are added to an ecosystem, it becomes increasingly complex. Younger children may need to see colored pictures similar to the pictures of the animals they are asked to color. (Otherwise you may get purple ground squirrels!)

The existence of an ecosystem is directly related to energy and its transfer. The sun is the major source of energy. Lower forms of plants and animals spend

FIGURE 116-1

FIGURE 116-2

FIGURE 116-3

most of their lives in producing and consuming energy. Reproducing the species, in many cases, is the only other function they perform. Some more advanced species do spend time in play.

The next activity introduces the concept of food chains and food webs, which form the basis for ecosystems.

# ACTIVITY 117: How Is Energy Transferred in an Ecosystem?

## *MATERIALS NEEDED*

- Complete grassland ecosystem from Activity 116
- Simple food chain chart (Figure 117-1)
- Simple food web (Figure 117-2)

## *PROCEDURE*

1. Study the picture of the grassland ecosystem. Energy from the sun is the basis of all life in the system. Why? Discuss this with your teacher and other members of the group.
2. Figure 117-1 is a diagram of a simple *food chain* showing how energy from the sun is used and stored in food molecules manufactured by the producers from nonliving materials. In turn, they are consumed by primary and secondary consumers. The waste products and remains of dead animals and plants are returned to the soil, where the scavangers and decomposers complete the cycle so that it can begin again.
3. There are many different ways food chains can work. Some consumers eat only certain producers. Other consumers eat both primary and secondary consumers. Weather and chemicals produced from the nonliving portions of the ecosystem (air, water, soil) also influence conditions within the system. Ecologists call these many variables the *food web*. Just as a spider spins a web one strand at a time, food webs are made up of many food chains. Compare the food web (Figure 117-2) with the food chain (Figure 117-1).

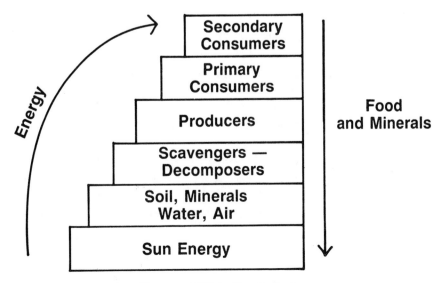

FIGURE 117-1. Food chain.

**Simple Food Web**

FIGURE 117-2. Food web.

4. Can you think of other ways chance might change the food web? What would happen if there were no mice?
5. Ecosystems are very complex. Can you see why ecology is an interesting and exciting science?

## *TEACHER INFORMATION*

Figures 117-1 and 117-2 have been simplified but should still give students a feeling for the highly complex interrelationships that occur in nature. Also, chance is always part of the interplay.

Using charts may convey a feeling of a static process. Ecosystems are actually highly dynamic, with countless variables. Students may need additional experience in constructing ecosystems and applying them to life situations. Later in the section, parks, vacant lots, and even back alley ecosystems will be discussed.

Show the Walt Disney film "Nature's Half Acre."

The next activity introduces the most complex variable in ecology—people.

# ACTIVITY 118: Where Do People Fit into an Ecosystem?

## *MATERIALS NEEDED*

- 3' × 6' poster of Figure 118-1
- Cutouts of plants and animals, such as Figures 116-1, 116-2, and 116-3
- Colored pencils

- Pictures of people, houses, stores, domestic animals, and so on
- Thumbtacks
- Drawing paper

## *PROCEDURE*

1. Study the picture on the large bulletin board. This is the way your community may have looked before the settlers came.
2. Identify the nonliving and living elements that make up the ecosystem.
3. Add a family to the system. What will they need to survive? Where will they get what they need?
4. Put a house and yard in the picture. Add a barn and barnyard. What animals will live in the barnyard? Where will the people get food? Plant crops?
5. Add a second family with all the things the first family has.
6. What is happening to the ecosystem?
7. Add a third house, family, and barn.
8. Build a general store, church, school, and post office near the homes.
9. Is this still an ecosystem?
10. What changes could you make in it? Discuss planning as a part of urban and suburban change.

## *TEACHER INFORMATION*

Figure 118-1 is a bulletin board developed from a grassland-woodland area. In representing more arid or humid regions, you can vary the environment and the people according to conditions. Be sure to have cutouts ready as you add people and houses.

Some teachers who like to sketch have used light pastels and drawn figures and objects in darker colors as the housing develops. The wild animals, fish, trees, bushes will need to be removable or be covered by cutouts. Involve students in the development of these materials if possible.

If you live in a large city or suburban area, the bulletin board as shown in Figure 118-1 could finally be covered by a tall skyline or rambling homes.

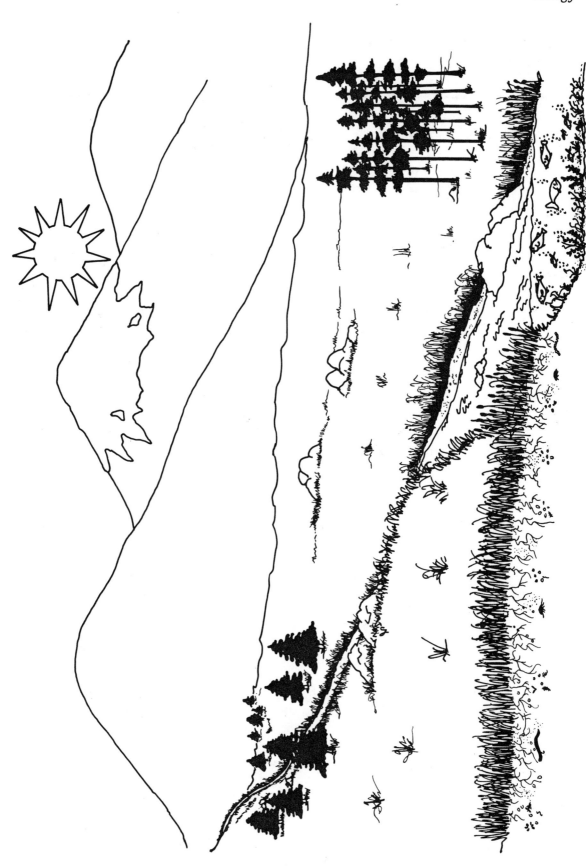

FIGURE 118-1. Grassland-woodland ecosystem.

The purpose of the activity is *not* to show how people destroy natural ecosystems. Rather, it should help students understand that with civilization natural ecosystems will change and that planning can help society preserve, conserve, and restore many ecosystems in the world. People are second-level consumers. As such, they have responsibilities to ecosystems if they are to continue to be supported by those systems. Remind the students of the picture of the earth as taken by astronauts on the moon.

Show the Walt Disney film "Large Animals That Once Roamed the Plains."

# ACTIVITY 119:  How Do You Fit into a Personal Ecosystem?

(Class discussion)

## *MATERIALS NEEDED*

- 9" × 12" paper
- Colored pencils
- Ruler

## *PROCEDURE*

1. We have learned how the ecosystem of your community has changed with time. Whether you live in a very small community or a very large metropolitan area, many things have changed, are changing, and will change. In the center of your paper make a small picture of yourself.
2. Next to you make a picture of the people (family) with whom you live and any animals you own.
3. Place a rectangle around your picture. This represents the place where you live and is the first part of your personal "ecosystem."
4. Somewhere near your home, make a picture of your favorite outdoor place to play (yard, park, playground, friends' yard, or alley). This is a second portion of your personal ecosystem.
5. Make a picture of your school with your classroom located in it. This is a third part of your personal ecosystem.
6. Next, draw small pictures of other places where you spend time regularly (church, club, friends' places, grandparents' or other relatives' places).
7. Make boxes around all the pictures and draw lines connecting your "home" box with all the others. Estimate the amount of time you spend with each of the elements each week and write the time in hours and minutes if you can.
8. You are a second-level consumer, and this web of boxes and lines represents most of the "ecosystem" in which you live.

## *TEACHER INFORMATION*

You will probably need to use the chalkboard or overhead projector to show how to construct the web. Younger children will be unable to estimate time spent, and perhaps distance, but the size of the pictures they draw could substitute for length of time and importance to them. It is best not to "model" family size or structure by drawing in two parents, other children, and so forth.

The web, of course, is not intended to represent any type of true ecosystem. Its purpose is to provide focus for the following activities, which will be centered around individuals and their relationships to people and things around them.

# ACTIVITY 120:  How Do You Live at Home?

## MATERIALS NEEDED

- 9″ × 12″ paper
- Crayons
- Ruler
- Pencil

## PROCEDURE

1. Draw an outline of your home. Divide your home into rooms or living areas. Choose your favorite color and mark the space that belongs to you. If you share a bedroom, color your part of the room.
2. Use different colors to show places that belong to other members of the family alone.
3. Some spaces are shared with others in your family. Use different colors to show "community" areas.
4. Animals who live together in communities within an ecosystem have rules that govern their own space or territory and territory shared with others. With other animals, most rules for community living are controlled by *instincts*—unlearned behavior that is beyond their personal control. Insect communities such as bees and ants live in a complex social structure controlled by instinctive behavior. In human communities, most behavior is controlled by thinking or reasoning—by rules.
5. On your paper make a small colored line to identify the territories (areas or rooms) in your home and write several rules for living and sharing in each territory.
6. Look at the rules you have written. Are they different for your personal territory, that shared by other members of your family, and guest territory if you have any?
7. Save this picture for a later activity.

## TEACHER INFORMATION

The following series of activities will attempt to help the student identify his or her place in various communities. The use of terms such as family, community, and ecosystem may help students realize that, just as with other animal relationships, they too have rights and responsibilities.

A positive approach to the use of rules instead of instincts should help children understand that they are necessary and helpful for survival, protection, and comfort.

Discuss and compare rules and family life styles with your class. Accept and positively reinforce differences. Help students understand reasons for the rights, responsibilities, and rules in their family community.

Several films or videocassette tapes of animal communities would be helpful to begin the class discussion. Films from the *True Life Adventure Series* produced by Walt Disney Studios should intitiate interesting comparisons. Try "Bear Country" or "Beaver Valley" before you begin the class discussion and comparisons. The results are often stimulating and exciting.

# ACTIVITY 121: How Do You Live in Your Classroom?

## MATERIALS NEEDED

- 9″ × 12″ paper
- Pencil
- Crayons
- Ruler

## PROCEDURE

1. Use your ruler to draw an outline of your classroom.
2. Locate and color your personal space in the classroom.
3. Mark and color your teacher's personal territory in the room.
4. Use another color to show the personal space of other students in the room.
5. Look around the room and decide what is shared space in your classroom community. Draw pictures of and color the shared territory. If there is any space not being used, leave it blank.
6. Think about the nonliving parts of your classroom environment. How do you get light, moisture, and air? Is the temperature comfortable for community living? Under your picture write a word or sentence to describe the nonliving parts of your classroom.
7. Since there are probably more members in your classroom community than your home, what additional rules are necessary?
8. On your paper list several important rules everyone needs to follow in order to live comfortably with others.
9. Discuss and compare your picture and rules with those of other members of the class.
10. Save your picture for use in a later activity.

## TEACHER INFORMATION

In any community, rules work only if they are understood, accepted, and supported by each individual. Even very young children need to understand reasons for community rules. In animal communities, the rules of instinct have probably developed from survival through natural selection. People have extended rules far beyond the instinctive survival level. Customs, traditions, mores, taboos, and religious beliefs are often translated into some kind of pattern of rules or laws with which a society is governed.

View the Walt Disney film *Seal Island* or *Flash, the Teenage Otter*.

# ACTIVITY 122: How Does Our School Community Function?

(Class discussion and small groups)

## MATERIALS NEEDED

- 24" × 36" chart paper
- Paper
- Pencils
- Portable tape recorders

## PROCEDURE

1. This activity may take several days to complete. With your teacher and other members of the class, make a drawing of your school. Show the classrooms and other spaces such as the library, lunchroom, auditorium, multipurpose room, offices, teachers' room, custodial areas, and lavatories. If your school has special features that you like, be sure to put them in.
2. Form small groups (four or five people) and choose an area (territory) of your school community you would like to study. List people you'd like to talk to and special things to look for in your area. Share the list with your teacher. Prepare some questions to ask about your area. Be sure to ask how students can help support this part of the school community. Ask about problems that are of special importance in that territory.
3. Make an appointment with the person in charge of the area you have chosen (librarian, principal, custodian, lunchroom manager, school secretary) and arrange an on-site visit. Be sure to take paper and a tape recorder so you will be able to report to your class.
4. After your visit, meet as a group and ask your teacher to help you prepare a brief report for the class. Include pictures and drawings.
5. Share your reports with the class. As other groups report, compare your findings with theirs.
6. Save all your material and notes for a later activity.

## TEACHER INFORMATION

Before you begin, be sure to discuss this activity with your principal and other members of the school staff who may be involved. Enlist their help in identifying special features and problems of their roles.

Students should realize that a well-functioning school community depends on the quality of each segment. A theme for this study might be "How do you help us? How can we help you?"

Be sure the students have specific questions to ask and that they gather data for a report. As a part of the report, school staff members might be willing to visit.

Visualizing the whole school on a chart (step 1) may be difficult for younger children (some adults, too). Before you use the 24″ × 36″ chart for class discussion, you may want to rule a light outline in pencil and use a black marker during the actual class discussion.

Teachers of young children may want to adapt this activity for the total group and develop it over a period of several weeks. (See Activity 124.)

# ACTIVITY 123: How Is Your School Like an Ecosystem?

## *MATERIALS NEEDED*

- Pictures of grassland ecosystem developed in Activity 114 (one per student)
- 24" × 36" poster
- 9" × 12" paper
- Pencil

## *PROCEDURE*

1. Look at your picture of a grassland ecosystem. Remember the important nonliving and living elements in it?
2. How is your school like an ecosystem? On your paper, make an outline of your school building.
3. Instead of a sun to provide energy, make a circle above the building and call it "Learning."
4. Inside the building, write the name of the major consumer of "learning."
5. Inside the building write the names of the major producers of learning.
6. Near the outside of the building write the names of organisms (people) who help the producers and consumers.
7. Farther away from the building write the names of nonliving things that help the producers and consumers.
8. Still farther away write the names of migratory producers who help but are not a permanent part of the system.
9. Can you think of other things that need to be added to the ecosystem? If so, put them in.
10. Compare your school "ecosystem" with a grassland ecosystem. Which do you think is more difficult to keep balanced?

## *TEACHER INFORMATION*

This activity is suggested with apologies to any purists in the field of ecology. There are many microecosystems within the school building and on the school grounds. However, the purpose of this analogy is to focus on the students' role in a system that functions to assist them. It is not unlike farmers and some large industries that use resources to provide consumer products. Most of these industries recognize their responsibilities to the ecological system on which they depend.

The following activity will help students identify specific problems in the school "ecosystem" and devise methods to solve some of them.

Figure 123-1 is a suggested model for your 24" × 36" poster. Modify it to fit your own situation.

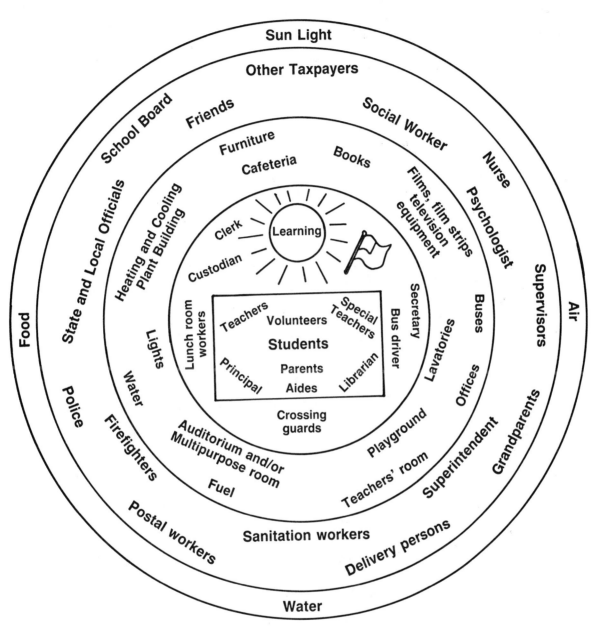

FIGURE 123-1. The school as an ecosystem.

# ACTIVITY 124:  How Can You Help an Ecosystem?

(Class discussion)

## MATERIALS NEEDED

- Group report materials from Activity 122
- Model of school "ecosystem" in Activity 123
- Newsprint
- Pencils

## PROCEDURE

1. This activity will take several days. Divide into the same groups you were in for Activity 122.
2. As a group, study the report you gave. Where do the problems you identified fit in the model of the school ecosystem?
3. If they are inside or close to the building, they are problems you can help solve.
4. Choose one simple problem and make a plan to help solve it (food waste in lunchroom, litter on school grounds, or similar problem.) Discuss the plan with your teacher.
5. Contact the person in charge of the area where the problem exists and talk about your plan. Try to plan long-term solutions so the problem won't keep happening again.
6. Plan some way of reporting the results of your efforts.
7. What might happen if all the people tried to solve little problems in the "ecosystem" in which they live?
8. In Activity 120 you studied the place where you live as a "community." Could the things you did at school help solve problems in your home?

## TEACHER INFORMATION

Following through with a plan of action is the most important segment of this series of activities. Research has shown that information has little effect on behavioral change unless it is translated into tangible action. This is especially important for students in the early and middle years.

Emphasize that it is more important to do something rather than everything. Each individual can restore or preserve some small part of the ecosystem where he or she is.

Step 8 asks the students to examine their "home community." The extent to which you explore this topic should depend on your judgment of the circumstances where you are. Accept "home community" to be whatever it is to the student.

Teachers of young children who are not ready for committee work should continue with a focus on one area and one problem as identified in Activity 122.

# ACTIVITY 125: How Can We Improve Our Environment?

(Teacher-conducted activity)

## MATERIALS NEEDED

- Tape recorder and tape with harsh noises
- Very interesting short story
- Paper
- Pencil

## PROCEDURE

1. Prepare a tape of loud music or noise of some kind.
2. Select a short but engrossing story appropriate to the age level of your students. A short film or VCR could be substituted.
3. As you reach the most interesting part of the story, turn the noise on loudly enough to drown out the narration.
4. Turn the sound off and finish the story.
5. Discuss the following:
   a. How did you feel when noise intruded on the story?
   b  Noise is a form of pollution.
   c. Noise is a health problem (ear damage from very loud music; see "Hearing" in your encyclopedia).
   d. Much noise pollution is unintentional. Some cannot be avoided. Think of examples of both kinds.
   e. How can personal awareness reduce noise pollution?
   f. If you want to listen to music in public, how can you do so without disturbing others?
   g. In a discussion with friends, do you occasionally talk more loudly so people will listen?
   h. Think of five people you like best. Are they noisy, average, or quiet people?
   i. Are you a listener or a talker or do you do an equal amount of both?
   j. How can you reduce your noise level?
   k. How can you reduce the noise level around you?
   l. Make an action plan of things you can do now to reduce noise pollution.

## TEACHER INFORMATION

This activity is the first of several to help students become aware of problems we face as we live together in a "human community." (Supporting activities can be found in Section 5, "Sound," of Book 2 of the Library.)

# ACTIVITY 126:  What Is Litter?

## *MATERIALS NEEDED*

- Garbage bags
- 24" × 36" poster (one per committee)
- Glue
- Tongs (one set per committee)

- Clean cotton gloves (one pair per committee)
- Plastic-covered table

## *PROCEDURE*

1. Divide into groups of four or five.
2. Choose an area near the school building such as the school grounds, curbs (not street), vacant lots, or sidewalk.
3. Take a garbage bag and spend thirty minutes collecting all materials that are not part of the natural environment in the area. Use the gloves or tongs to pick up things that are sharp or dirty. (Don't collect or touch dead animals.)
4. After 30 minutes, return to class with the things you have collected.
5. Put everything on a plastic-covered table. Can you find ways to classify or organize them?
6. Use the poster paper and glue to make three-dimensional collages of the material.
7. Think of titles or slogans for the pictures.
8. Display them in your room and other parts of the school.
9. Wash your hands frequently during this activity.
10. The area you picked up is clean now. How could you keep it that way?

## *TEACHER INFORMATION*

This activity is regularly used in schools. It seems most effective when the goal is to sensitize students to litter and how easily it accumulates. The most important message should be that each bit of litter represents a careless, lazy, or thoughtless person. Many careless, lazy, thoughtless people produce an ugly, littered, and often unhealthy environment. Students should realize that they, as individuals, are responsible for the control of litter.

The Walt Disney movie "The Litterbug" is an excellent film to show at this time. It provides additional specific reinforcement and topics for additional discussion.

# ACTIVITY 127: How Can We Involve Others?

## *MATERIALS NEEDED*

- Clean garbage can or large wastebaskets
- Plastic dropcloths
- Paintbrushes
- Tempera paints

## *PROCEDURE*

1. We have seen that noise pollution and litter begin with individuals. Most people will attempt to control these problems if they become aware of them and are given help. Divide into small committees and find a clean wastebasket or garbage can.
2. Plan a picture or slogan to paint on the can to attract other people's attention. Remember you want to attract attention and get people to use the garbage can.
3. Use bright tempera paint to decorate the cans.
4. Put them in special places in the school to attract attention.
5. With your teacher, discuss the possibility of challenging another classroom or even the whole school to a wastebasket-decorating contest.

## *TEACHER INFORMATION*

Simple, brightly painted cans are best. Be sure you have the approval of your principal and custodian before undertaking this project.

This type of activity will be most effective if the focus is kept on the individual, such as by using the word "you" in the slogan.

Perhaps your PTA would be willing to offer a prize for the best garbage can (or better yet, *all* cans).

# ACTIVITY 128:  What Is a Wise Consumer?

## *MATERIALS NEEDED*

- Pictures of a modern grocery store or supermarket
- Paper
- Pencil

## *PROCEDURE*

1. With your teacher plan a trip to a nearby grocery store.
2. Ask the store owner to show you all the things sold in the store that could not be purchased 25 years ago, 50 years ago, and 100 years ago. Find out how many products are biodegradable.
3. Make a four-column list of things available 100 years ago, 50 years ago, 25 years ago, and today.
4. Look at the containers newer things come in. Ask the manager to tell you about them. Find out about sale dating.
5. When you return to your school, compare your lists. How have containers improved our lives? How has modern food handling improved our lives? What effect have these had on ecology?
6. Would you be willing to give up the modern products to have a cleaner environment?
7. Can you think of ways you could help with this problem?

## *TEACHER INFORMATION*

A grocery store or even a neighborhood fast-food establishment or delicatessen can be a rich source for studies in many areas. Ecology, economics, merchandising, service, and courtesy are topics to be studied in most stores. Old-time general merchandise stores still exist in small communities. The suburban shopping center is simply the enlargement and modernization of the same concept. In large cities, the relationship of people to the deli operator is similar to that of the people in a small town to the owner of the general store.

Someone in your class may have a relative who owns or works in a grocery store. Make a personal visit in advance and leave a written list of specific topics you would like covered during the class visit.

Although the major topics will be packing, conservation, and food handling as related to ecology, watch for other learning opportunities for return visits.

Emphasize that the great benefits of modern packaging and handling also create additional problems in garbage disposal and littering.

# ACTIVITY 129: What Changes Have Happened Where You Live?

## MATERIALS NEEDED

- Two or three older people who have lived in your community for many years
- Paper
- Pencil
- Tape recorder

## PROCEDURE

1. Survey the class and identify two or three older people who have lived in your community for a long time.
2. As a class, make a list of questions you would like to ask about changes in the ecology of the region.
3. Contact the people and invite them to attend class and answer the questions. Be sure to ask them to bring old pictures or other items they may have to show. Emphasize that you are interested in changes in the physical environment of your community.
4. When your guests arrive, be prepared to ask specific questions about changes in ecology.

## TEACHER INFORMATION

Older people can be excellent sources of special information about your community. They often know of places in parks, yards of older homes, and even cemeteries where vestiges of the past still exist. Mutual lasting bonds are often formed from these visits.

# ACTIVITY 130: Do You Conserve Your Resources Wisely?

(Total class discussion)

## MATERIALS NEEDED

- All clothing and other items from the school's "lost-and-found"
- Some item from home that is usable but that you have outgrown or no longer need or want
- Paper
- Pencil

## PROCEDURE

1. Look at the items in the school "lost-and-found" box. How many of the materials are still usable?
2. Why do you think they are there?
3. Can you think of a way to solve this problem?
4. Show the item you brought from home to the other class members.
5. Trade as many items as you can with other members of the class.
6. Perhaps some items left over could be used for another purpose.
7. Play the "What can you do with an old _____?" game. One person says "What can you do with an old _____?" and quickly holds up a leftover item. Everyone writes down as many things as he or she can think of in one minute. The one who has the longest list wins that item and has the chance to choose and hold up the next item. Continue this until everything is gone. At the end of class, if you *really* don't want the item you have won, give it to your decorated garbage can. It wants everything!
8. Return the lost-and-found items to the principal with any suggestions you have for their disposal.

## TEACHER INFORMATION

Your school may have another solution for lost-and-found articles, or it may have been one of the problems you studied earlier when you developed the school as an ecosystem. If so, begin with step 4.

The purpose of this activity is to help students become aware of how much we, as consumers, waste. "Use it up, wear it out, make it do" was the slogan that many people lived by a century ago. Today, in an age of plenty, it's easy for some to overlook the days before modern technology relieved much of the survival-level existence that was common in this country. In many parts of this country and in much of the world, survival-level living is still common. If you live or teach in such an area, this activity can have even more meaning.

# ACTIVITY 131: How Can You Reuse Newspaper?

## *MATERIALS NEEDED*

- Newspapers
- Mixing bowl
- Wallpaper paste or liquid laundry starch
- Table, board, or cake pan
- Wax paper
- Eggbeater
- Water
- Window screen
- Glass jar or drinking glass

## *PROCEDURE*

1. Begin with a piece of newspaper about 20 cm. (1 ft.) square.
2. Cut or tear the newspaper into small pieces.
3. Place the pieces of paper in the mixing bowl, add a cup of water, and let it sit for a few minutes so the water will soak completely through the paper.
4. Churn the paper and water with the egg beater until the paper is broken up into very small pieces and the mixture looks something like rolled oats cereal.
5. Add one tablespoon of wallpaper paste or laundry starch. (If the wallpaper paste or starch is in powder form, mix it with a little water before adding it to the batch.)
6. Stir the mixture well.
7. Lay the window screen on a table, board, or inverted cake pan.
8. Spread the mixture into a thin layer on the screen.
9. Lay a sheet of waxed paper over the mixture and roll a fruit jar or a drinking glass over it to squeeze out the excess water.
10. Carefully remove the waxed paper and allow the mixture to dry. It will probably need a day or two.
11. When the mixture is thoroughly dry, remove it from the screen carefully. You have made a usable product from waste material. This idea of reusing is called *recycling*.
12. Clean up the screen for use again.

## *TEACHER INFORMATION*

It is estimated that about half the solid waste in the cities and towns of this nation consists of paper and paper products. Recycling of this material is an important industry and a worthy effort. Enough paper is recycled to save the lives of millions of trees each year. The paper produced by this activity is not exactly refined paper for your notebook, but it is definitely paper. Besides, it is done by the student and the process is quite like that done on a larger scale by paper industries.

# ACTIVITY 132:  Which Solids Decompose Easily?

---

## *MATERIALS NEEDED*

- Large, deep tray, such as a suit box
- Plastic liner or plastic garbage bag
- Water
- Soil
- Samples of small items (solid waste) out of garbage cans
- Paper
- Pencil

## *PROCEDURE*

1. Line the box with the plastic.
2. Put a layer of soil about 3–5 cm. (1–2 in.) deep in the bottom of the box. Spread it out so it is uniform.
3. Place your samples of solid waste around on top of the layer of soil.
4. Make a "map" on paper, showing which items you used and where they were placed on the tray.
5. Cover the items with another layer of soil about the same thickness as the first.
6. Sprinkle some water on it, enough to wet the soil.
7. Let the box sit for a period of four to six weeks. Sprinkle a little bit of water on it each day or so to keep the soil moist.
8. When the time period is up, remove the top layer of soil and check the samples.
9. Refer to the map you made in step 4 so each item can be located easily. Record the amount of decomposition of each item.
10. Which items decomposed the most? What were they made of?
11. Which items decomposed the least? What were they made of?

## *TEACHER INFORMATION*

The average solid waste in the United States has been estimated at about 5.3 pounds per person per day. Have some students use that rate to figure out the amount for your school, city, state, or nation. Much of this waste material is hauled to sanitary landfills and covered with dirt. Sometimes it is crushed first. After it is covered with soil, bacteria and moisture begin their work of decomposing the material. However, some of the solids don't cooperate very well. Such materials are very difficult to completely dispose of. To keep our environment clean, materials that become garbage must either be recycled or decomposed.

This activity is to give students a way to find out which materials will decompose readily and which will not. Samples used should be small and thin. Students could use a tin can lid, a piece of aluminum foil, a toothpick, a piece of a plastic bottle, various types of paper and fabric, a rubber band, and so on. They also need to be very patient. Decomposing matter by natural means requires a lot of time. At least four to six weeks should be allowed in order for changes to be observed.

# ACTIVITY 133: How Can You Make a Water Treatment Plant?

## *MATERIALS NEEDED*

- Tin can
- Two shallow cake pans
- Board, slightly longer than the width of one pan
- Sand

- Small rocks
- Rubber or plastic tubing 45 cm. (18 in.) long
- Metal puncher
- Several books or sturdy box
- Muddy water

## *PROCEDURE*

1. Punch two or three small holes near the bottom of the can.
2. Wash the sand and the small rocks and be sure the can is clean.
3. Put sand in the can until it is about half full. Add small rocks until the can is about three-fourths full. This is the filter.
4. Place the board across the top of one of the pans and put the can on the board. The can should be placed so the drain holes in the can are off one edge of the board for free drainage.
5. Put the other pan on a stack of books or other support so the bottom of it is slightly above the top of the can. This is the *settling basin*.

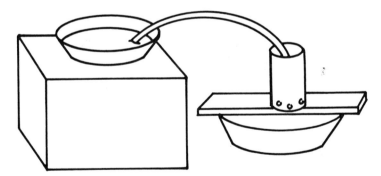

FIGURE 133-1. Water treatment plant ready for use.

6. Pour muddy water into the settling basin and let it settle for an hour or more.
7. Using the tubing as a siphon base, siphon some of the water slowly from the settling basin to the filter and allow it the time needed to drain through the filter.
8. As the water drips out of the filter and into the pan, compare it with the water in the settling basin.

## TEACHER INFORMATION

Before beginning this activity, explain to the students that many cities use lakes and reservoirs for their culinary water supply. This water must be purified in order to make it safe for drinking and cooking. Water treatment plants are an important service to the people.

The water treatment plant constructed in this activity is a fairly effective system for filtering muddy water. If it has been constructed properly, water from the filter will be clear. Have students try filtering some salt water with it. They could test the purity of the salt water by tasting it or by evaporting a small amount of the filtered water from a jar to find out if a salt residue remains in the jar. A similar amount of unfiltered salt water should be evaporated from another jar for comparison. Report what happens.

A field trip to a water treatment plant or a sewage plant would be timely and valuable in connection with this activity. If this is not possible, perhaps a note home suggesting such an outing for the family would result in some of the students having the experience.

# ACTIVITY 134: What Have We Learned?

(Total-class activity)

## *MATERIALS NEEDED*

- Folders of materials developed during the ecology study
- Pictures, charts, and bulletin boards
- Resource persons

## *PROCEDURE*

1. As a class, plan an "awareness day" so you can share what you have learned with others.
2. Decide what you would like to show and how you will do it.
3. Who should be invited?
4. How can you involve and inform them?
5. To help you in your planning, look at the following ideas:
   a. Tell about the display, the notes, and the pictures you made as you studied ecology.
   b. Have a clothing (glove, boot) exchange table.
   c. Make bumper stickers with "-ives" on them, such as "Dirt is abras*ive*, noise is intrus*ive*, salt is corros*ive*."
   d. Display "new" things you have made out of "old" things.
   e. Create a "Lucy and Larry Litterbug" play. Make it into a VCR and invite others to view it.
   f. Learn and sing some songs about ecology and a beautiful earth.
   g. Serve school-grown foods.
   h. Make litter bags and give them to others to use.
   i. Display "prize-winning" wastebaskets and garbage cans.
   j. Invite resource people from the community to attend and display some of their materials.
   k. Show parts of the favorite film or VCR you used during your study.
   l. Think of more ideas to add to this list. Do them!
6. When this final activity is over, be sure you leave your environment neat and clean.

## *TEACHER INFORMATION*

An "awareness day" will help the students organize the materials and reinforce what they have learned during the study.

Involvement of other people, parents, and classes will require the cooperation of your faculty and principal.

*Section 7*

---

*ABOVE THE EARTH*

# TO THE TEACHER

Suppose a small child at play on the beach at Kitty Hawk, North Carolina, had paused to watch the first flight of Orville and Wilbur Wright. Less than seventy years later, that same individual could have watched on television as the first man walked on the moon. The incredible and fascinating story of flight above the earth is introduced in this section.

To help students understand and appreciate the progress of the human race in the twentieth century, a brief background is presented as Activity 135. You are invited to read and discuss it with your class. Tape record it for small-group discussions, have it read individually or, if you prefer, choose an alternate method with your librarian or media specialist.

Learning to simulate controlled flight can be exciting and enjoyable. You may even find yourself helping to build a large cardboard mock-up of a pilot's cockpit with simulated controls. (If, as a result of these activities, you decide to fly a real airplane or space ship, we strongly recommend that you take additional lessons first.)

The following activities are offered to help you and your students learn about our remarkable progress in the quest to move into the unknown, and perhaps to challenge some of you to dream of what lies beyond.

# ACTIVITY 135: What Is the History of Flight?

## *MATERIALS NEEDED*

- Story of flight

## *PROCEDURE*

Read this story and discuss it with your classmates.

"One small step for man. One giant leap for mankind." Neil Armstrong's famous words as he took his first step on the moon marked an end and a beginning for man's desire to fly above the earth and beyond.

From earliest times human beings have seemed to want to follow the birds. We know there was at least one species of dinosaur that could fly *(pterosaur)* and an early ancestor of the modern feathered bird, called *Aechaeopteryx.* Myths, legends, and folklore tell of our continuing interest, and sometimes passion, to fly. A famous Greek legend tells about a boy named Icarus whose father gave him wings of feathers held together with wax to help him escape from his enemies. The wings worked, but while Icarus was flying he became careless and daring and flew too close to the sun. The sun's heat melted the wax that was holding the feathers together and Icarus fell into the sea.

For many centuries, people attempted to imitate birds by using their own muscles to power larger and larger wings.

Near the end of the fifteenth century a famous artist and inventor, Leonardo da Vinci, drew plans and pictures of a manpowered machine for flight. There is no record that his design was ever constructed or tested.

For another 300 years, birds, bats, insects, a few fish, and squirrels (flying) continued to be the only animals capable of rising above the earth's surface. The attempts of people to rise above the earth, using muscles as power, continued to fail time after time. People were too heavy, and their arms and legs were too weak.

Late in the eighteenth century, a Frenchman named Joseph Montgolfier watched burned ashes of paper rising above a fire and suddenly had an idea. Although he did not understand why hot air rises, he made a small bag of silk, built a fire under it, and watched it fly away. Later, he and his brother constructed a large balloon, built a fire under it, and it lifted a man above the earth for the first time. Soon afterward, balloons filled with hydrogen gas were developed. The scientific principle of displacement use in "lighter than air" ballooning was discovered by a greek scientist, Archimedes, in about 300 B.C.

Ballooning became popular as a sport. Some practical uses were developed for balloons, but because they were so fragile and difficult to control, their use did not become widespread. People still studied birds for an answer to practical flight.

Near the beginning of the nineteenth century, an Englishman named George Cayley discovered the first principles that would lead to controlled flight as we know it today. By watching birds, Cayley realized they work very hard to get into the air but once airborne, most were able to glide and fly using very little energy.

Cayley became interested in how, for many birds, staying in the air required so little effort. He decided something must be holding them up. Using information about the pressure of moving air, Cayley was able to design and build the first successful glider that soared above the earth. Late in the nineteenth century, a German engineer named Otto Lilienthal developed methods to control glider flight, controlled power flight became a possibility.

Before people could fly under power, they needed a simple, lightweight source of energy. Steam engines used in the nineteenth century were too heavy. Attempts to use them for powered flight always failed and often ended in disaster. The small, lightweight internal combustion (gasoline) engine seemed to offer a possible alternative to muscle power, which was not strong enough, and steam, which was not light enough.

At the beginning of the twentieth century, American brothers Orville and Wilbur Wright, began experimenting with gliders on a windy beach at Kitty Hawk, North Carolina. On December 17, 1903, the first powered flight was made. Human beings had finally learned how to control and power flight.

Since that time, progress has been rapid. Airflight was adapted to transportation, communication, and even warfare. During the 1930s and 1940s a different source of power, rocket energy, was introduced and developed. For many centuries the Chinese, Greeks, and others had known about rocket propulsion but it was not until the middle of the twentieth century that it was seriously studied as energy for manned flight.

Before 1960, the Russians put a small satellite in orbit around the earth. The first rocket-powered space flight came soon after.

For the next 10 years, step by step, flight after flight, test after test, human beings gradually climbed the ladder to the moon. Who knows what lies beyond?

Someday, some of you may follow the countless generations of people who wanted to fly. You are the astronauts, the explorers of the future!

## TEACHER INFORMATION

Have your students read this story or read it to them. You may want to come back to the story as you proceed through this section.

Before beginning these activities, you should review Activities 9 and 18 from Section 1, "Starter Ideas," and Activities 35 and 36 from Section 2, "Air."

# ACTIVITY 136: What Is a Wind Tunnel?

(Teacher-supervised activity)

## MATERIALS NEEDED

- Variable speed fans
- Cardboard boxes with dividers (must be larger than the fans)
- Ruler
- Utility knife
- Paper

## PROCEDURE

1. For the following activities, you will need a controlled source of wind. Scientists and engineers use wind tunnels to test air currents around shapes they design. Remove the top of the cardboard box and lay the box on its side.
2. Measure the diameter of the fan and cut a hole in the bottom of the box about the same size. This will control the air from the fan and conduct it through the box.
3. Put the fan behind the box and turn it on.
4. Holding a flat piece of paper by the edges, move it in front of the box.
5. If the paper behaves the same as the one you used to test Bernoulli's principle (see Activity 18), your wind tunnel is a success!

FIGURE 136-1. Wind tunnel.

## TEACHER INFORMATION

For the following activities, you will need to borrow several fans and make several wind tunnels. Box fans are designed to be a type of wind tunnel, but because of their size, they often produce too much air. Eight- to 12-inch fans with variable speeds are ideal. If they oscillate, there is usually an adjustment to stop them. Boxes with many small dividers are better than ones designed to hold gallon containers.

This activity assumes completion of Activity 18 as suggested in "Teacher Information" of Activity 135.

# ACTIVITY 137:  How Does Shape Affect Lift?

## *MATERIALS NEEDED*

- 5" × 7" index cards
- Cellophane tape
- Pencil
- Wind tunnel
- Fan

## *PROCEDURE*

1. Bend two cards slightly in the middle and tape them together.
2. Put a pencil between them.
3. Hold the pencil supporting the cards in front of the wind tunnel. Turn on the fan.
4. What happened?
5. Use other cards bent in different shapes to see which works best.
6. Label your best design "1" and give the highest number to the worst design. Mark each card.
7. Compare and discuss your findings with your teacher and classmates.

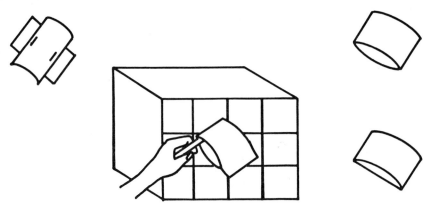

FIGURE 137-1. Pencil and cards being held in front of wind tunnel.

## *TEACHER INFORMATION*

This idea was introduced as Bernoulli's principle in Activity 18. Cayley, discussed in the story in Activity 135, discovered this same idea by watching birds.

When air moves over a curved surface, it goes faster, thereby reducing the pressure. A curved surface on the top of a wing reduces the air pressure above it and provides *lift*.

# ACTIVITY 138: How Can You Build a Simple Glider?

## *MATERIALS NEEDED*

- Strip of oak tag 20 cm. long × 8 cm. wide (8 in. × 3 in.)
- Two long, thin rubber bands
- Pencil

## *PROCEDURE*

1. Use the patterns in Figure 138-1 to cut two wings from the oak tag.
2. Fold the ends of the tail up and use a rubber band to attach it near one end of the pencil.
3. Use the other rubber band to attach the wing near the opposite end of the pencil.
4. Slide the wing back and forth until the middle of the pencil will balance on the side of your index finger.
5. If your glider looks like the illustration, it is ready for the wind tunnel test described in the next activity.

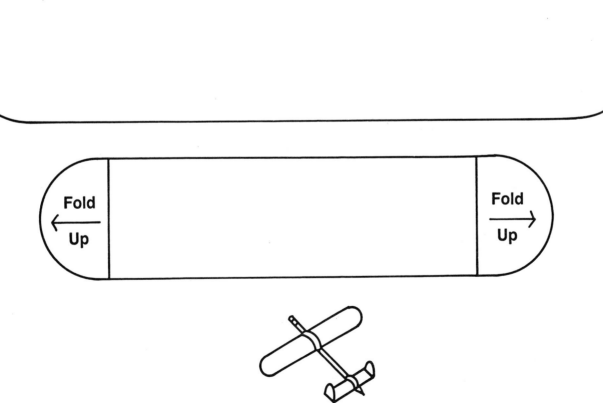

FIGURE 138-1. Wing and tail patterns and completed plane.

## TEACHER INFORMATION

You may need to help the children attach the wings to the gliders. Use hexagonal-sided pencils so the wing and tail will align easily.

# ACTIVITY 139: Will Your Airplane Soar?

## *MATERIALS NEEDED*

- Paper airplane constructed in Activity 138
- String 60 cm. (24 in.) long
- Cellophane tape
- Wind tunnel
- Fan

## *PROCEDURE*

1. As they are being designed, new airplanes are tested in some type of wind tunnel. Use cellophane tape to attach the ends of the string to the front and rear of your plane.
2. Hold the string so your plane is level and balanced. You may have to change the position of your hand on the string and adjust the wing until it is.
3. Turn the fan on low speed and carefully move your airplane in front of the wind tunnel. What happened?
4. Twist the string to the right. Twist the string to the left. Move your hand so the nose of the plane turns up. Move your hand so the nose turns down.
5. How can you describe the behavior of your plane in the wind?

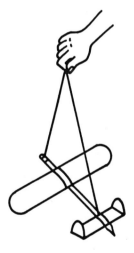

FIGURE 139-1. Airplane with string attached.

## TEACHER INFORMATION

If it is carefully balanced and aligned, the airplane will face the wind tunnel and maintain steady flight. Twisting the string will not turn the model because air passing the upright "rudders" on the tail section will hold it in line.

Lowering or raising the nose of the plane will cause broad, flat surfaces to be exposed to the wind and it may spin out of control.

The purpose of this wind tunnel activity is to help children realize that gliders need more than a wing and a tail if they are to be controlled.

# ACTIVITY 140: How Can We Turn Our Gliders?

## MATERIALS NEEDED

- Wind tunnel and fan
- Glider from Activity 141
- Scissors
- Ruler
- Newsprint
- Pencil

## PROCEDURE

1. Measure and carefully cut control surfaces in your glider as shown in Figure 140-1. Don't cut along dotted lines.
2. Follow the dotted lines to bend both rear sections of both rudders to the left. Hold your glider in front of the wind tunnel. What happened?
3. Try step 2 again, bending your rudders to the right. On your paper draw pictures of the glider showing right and left rudders.
4. Straighten the rudders. Bend the left aileron down along the dotted line and the right one up. Hold your glider in front of the wind tunnel. What happened?
5. Reverse the ailerons and try it again. Make two pictures of your glider showing what happened when you used the ailerons.
6. Find the best combination of rudders and ailerons to make your glider turn smoothly.

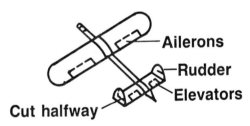

FIGURE 140-1. Glider with ailerons, rudders, and elevators marked.

## TEACHER INFORMATION

Rudders turn the glider left and right on a flat plane. Ailerons cause the wings to tilt or bank. With careful adjustment, the students should realize that a combination of banking with the ailerons and turning with the rudder will result in a smooth turn pattern.

# ACTIVITY 141: How Can We Make Our Glider Go Up and Down?

## MATERIALS NEEDED

- Same as for Activity 140

## PROCEDURE

1. Be sure the ailerons and rudder are straight. Test your glider in the wind tunnel to be sure it flies level and straight.
2. Remove your glider from the wind tunnel. Bend both elevators on the tail up.
3. Hang the loop of string attached to your glider over your index finger. Carefully move the glider in front of the wind tunnel. What happened?
4. Can you predict what will happen when you bend the elevator down? Try it.
5. Draw a side view of the glider showing what happens when you turn the elevators up and down.
6. Your glider now has the controls found in a simple airplane.

## TEACHER INFORMATION

Elevators use wind to push the tail up or down, thereby causing the nose of the glider to move in the opposite direction. Tail down, nose up (climb); tail up, nose down (descend). Too much tilt in the elevators will cause a stall (nose too high) or a dive (nose too low).

The following activities are designed to see how well children understand flight controls.

# ACTIVITY 142: What Have We Learned About Flying?

## *MATERIALS NEEDED*

- Student sketches of gliders from Activities 139 and 140
- Pencil

## *PROCEDURE*

1. Study the pictures of the three aircraft illustrated. In each of the pictures, the pilot is moving a control that will make a change in the position of the airplane.
2. Use the sketches of your glider that you made in Activities 139 and 140 to identify each change.
3. Draw arrows on each figure showing what will happen to the aircraft.
4. Compare your answers with those of others in the class. If your arrows were correct, you are ready to try a solo flight.

FIGURE 142-1. Aileron control movement.

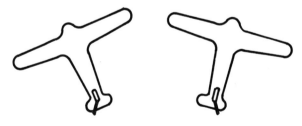

FIGURE 142-2. Rudder control movement.

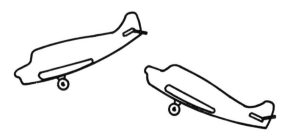

FIGURE 142-3. Elevator control movement.

## TEACHER INFORMATION

In Figure 142-1, the lowered aileron will force the wing upward. The arrows should point in the direction the aircraft is tilting. In Figure 142-2, the rudder forms a flat surface to push the tail in the opposite direction. Figure 142-3 shows the flat surface of the elevator turned down, forcing the tail up and the nose down, and vice versa. The figures show aircraft in the middle of the maneuver. The arrows should point in the same direction as the aircraft appears to be moving.

# ACTIVITY 143:  What Aircraft Will You Fly?

## *MATERIALS NEEDED*

- One piece of oak tag 20 cm. long × 8 cm. wide (8 in. × 3½ in.)
- One piece of oak tag 8 cm. long × 5 cm. wide (3½ in. × 2 in.)
- One piece of oak tag 5 cm. × 5 cm. (2 in. × 2 in.)

- Pencil with eraser
- Stapler
- Rubber cement
- Ruler
- Scissors
- Long, thin rubber band

## *PROCEDURE*

1. Shown here is a small picture of a larger "swept-wing supersonic" glider you can build. Look at the picture as you do the next steps.
2. Put the longest strip of oak tag across your desk. Put a dot in the center of the top 10 cm. (4 in.) from each corner.
3. From the bottom of each side, measure up 2 cm. (¾ in.) and put a dot.
4. Use your ruler to draw lines from the dots on the sides to the dot in the center. This is the leading edge of the wing of your glider.
5. From the center top, measure down 5 cm. (2 in.) and put a dot. Draw a line from each bottom corner to the dot. If your outline of a wing is similar to the one shown here, cut it out. Cut ailerons in each wing 2 cm. (¾ in.) from the end, 3 cm. (1 in.) long.
6. Use the larger of the two pieces of oak tag to make the elevator portion. Follow the same steps as you did to make the wing. The center top will be 4 cm. (1½ in.) from each end. Measure up 2 cm. (¾ in.) on each side and connect the dots to make the front edge. Measure down 3 cm. (1 in.) from the top center to make the center of the trailing edge. From this dot, draw lines to the lower corners. Cut your elevator out and cut movable tabs in it.
7. Put the small piece of oak tag under one half of the elevator. Trace it, cut it out, and make a tab in it. It will be the rudder.
8. Staple the elevator to a flat side of the bare end of the pencil.
9. Use rubber cement to glue the rudder upright on top of the elevator.
10. Use the rubber band to secure the wing near the eraser end of the pencil on the same flat surface as the tail section.
11. Move the wing forward or backward until the tips of the leading edges of the wing will balance on your outstretched index fingers.
12. Without moving any of the controls, try your plane in a very gentle glide. Adjust the wing position until it glides smoothly.
13. Test each of your controls, one at a time, to be sure they work properly.
14. If everything works, you are ready to demonstrate how well you can fly.

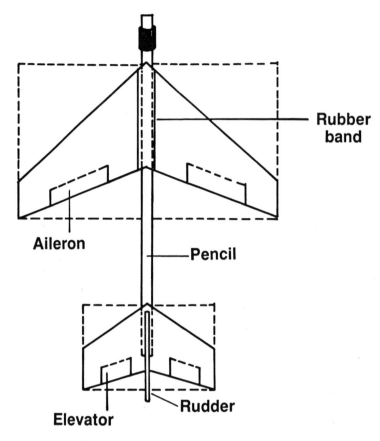

FIGURE 143-1. Swept-wing glider.

## TEACHER INFORMATION

Build and test a glider first before giving exact wing and tail measurements. You may need to increase the wing size. Exact measurements are not critical. The important factors will be balance and the ratio of wing and tail surfaces to weight. Bodies made of balsa wood or rolled oak tag weigh less but are not as sturdy and may need extra weight in the front.

If you, the students, or parents have different "favorite" paper airplanes, construct them. The only requirement should be that all aircraft have the three fundamental controls. Parental input should be limited to supplying interest, encouragement, and perhaps some assistance with the design.

# ACTIVITY 144: How Well Can You Fly?

## *MATERIALS NEEDED*

- Paper glider constructed in Activity 143
- String 10 m. (10 yds.) long
- Large ball

## *PROCEDURE*

1. Now that you have the knowledge and an aircraft, let's see how well you can fly. Choose a wide, flat area either indoors or out.
2. Put a large ball in the center of your area.
3. With one end of the string under the ball, make several spirals around the ball.
4. The spirals are your landing area, the ball is your target.
5. Stand at least 10 meters (10 yards) away and try to land your airplane on the target. Remember, you should analyze each flight and make adjustments in your controls for the next one.
6. Each time you hit the target, move back 5 meters (5 yards) and try again.
7. Have your teacher time you for 10 minutes.
8. At the end of the time, the pilots who are standing the greatest distance away are the "aces."

## *TEACHER INFORMATION*

This "just-for-fun" activity can mark the end of the flight section or, if interest is high you could purchase a large glider or kite and study air currents. A visit from a pilot (with visuals), a movie, or a field trip to an airport would be appropriate enrichment activities. The next series of investigations will help us begin a space adventure.

# ACTIVITY 145:  How Can a Ball Help You Move?

## *MATERIALS NEEDED*

- Heavy ball, such as a medicine ball or an old basketball stuffed with cloth
- Roller skates
- Water-soluble felt pen

## *PROCEDURE*

1. Put on the roller skates. Stand on a smooth, flat surface, skates parallel.
2. Have a friend mark the spot where the back rollers of your skates touch the floor and then stand in front of you, no closer than one meter (1 yard).
3. Hold the ball in both hands close to your chest. Throw it to your friend with a pushing motion.
4. Mark the position of the back rollers of your skates.
5. Repeat steps 3 and 4 several times.
6. What happened? What can you say about this?

## *TEACHER INFORMATION*

Each time the person on skates throws the ball in one direction *(action)* he or she will move in the opposite direction *(reaction)*. Newton stated this principle as his third law of motion: "For every action there is an equal and opposite reaction."

The student throwing the ball will not move the same distance as the ball travels due to other forces of friction and inertia. However, each time the ball is thrown in one direction, the person on skates will move an observable and measurable distance in the opposite direction.

# ACTIVITY 146: What Type of Energy Is This?

(Teacher-supervised activity)

## *MATERIALS NEEDED*

- Quart can
- Large nail
- Hammer
- Heavy string 1 m. (1 yd.) long
- One fishing swivel
- Scissors
- Sink
- Water

## *PROCEDURE*

1. Use the hammer and nail to punch four holes at equal distances around the can near the bottom edge. Drive the nail in at a steep angle so the holes appear semicircular. Be sure all holes point in the same direction.
2. Make three small holes around the top of the can (large enough for string).
3. Cut the string into four 25-cm (10-in.) lengths.
4. Tie one string to one end of the fishing swivel. Tie the other three strands to the other end.
5. Thread each of the three strings through a hole in the top of the can and tie them securely.
6. Hold your can over the sink at arm's length and have someone else pour water into it. Use the water tap at full force if it doesn't touch the string or can.
7. What happened? Can you explain why?

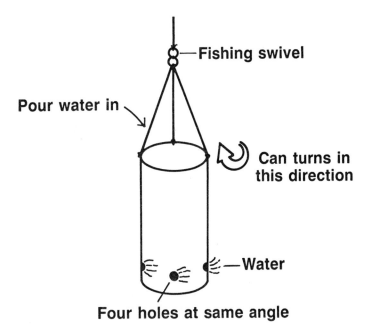

**Pour water in**

**Fishing swivel**

**Can turns in this direction**

**Water**

**Four holes at same angle**

Figure 146-1. Can with holes rotating on strings.

## *TEACHER INFORMATION*

This principle was discovered by a Greek named Heron of Alexandria nearly 2,000 years ago (see the encyclopedia).

There are other ways of helping children discover the principle of action-reaction. (for every action there is an equal and opposite reaction). One is to put an air gun (not BB) on a roller skate. Each time the air gun is fired in one direction, the skate and gun will move in the opposite direction *(recoil)*. A plastic medicine bottle with a snap top (not safety) may be placed on round pencils as rollers. Put a mixture of bicarbonate of soda and vinegar in the bottle and snap on the top. $CO_2$ gas will form inside the bottle, pop the top off, and move the bottle along the pencil rollers in the opposite direction of the popped cap. *(Note:* This is a very messy demonstration!)

# ACTIVITY 147: What Can a Marble Game Tell Us?

## *MATERIALS NEEDED*

- ½-in. garden hose cut in half lengthwise, 2 m. (2 yds.) long
- Marbles
- Two chairs

## *PROCEDURE*

1. Bend the half hose, open side up, into a nearly U shape between two chairs.
2. Put six marbles in the lowest part of the hose. Be sure they move freely.
3. While observing the marbles resting in the bottom of the hose, release one marble in the groove at the top of the hose. What happened?
4. Release two marbles at exactly the same time at the top of the groove. What happened at the bottom?
5. Try releasing different numbers of marbles. What happened? Can you explain why? Can you predict what would happen if you had more marbles?
6. What will happen if you have *two* marbles at the bottom and release three at the top? Try it.

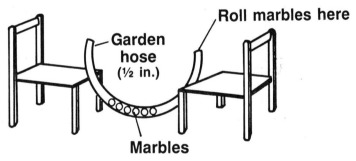

FIGURE 147-1. Garden hose placed between chairs.

## *TEACHER INFORMATION*

If you can obtain small ball bearings (round wheel bearings) and plastic or rubber tubing in half-meter lengths each student can construct this project. This is another investigation of action-reaction. When one marble is released in the groove at the top, it will roll down and strike the end marble in the row at the bottom. The marble at the opposite end of the row will move up the hose on the opposite side. If two marbles strike the row on one side, two will move away on the opposite side. If more marbles strike the row than there are marbles at rest, the nearest moving marble(s) will continue on with the ones set in motion. This is an excellent "take-home-and-tell-about" activity.

# ACTIVITY 148:  How Can We Use Action-Reaction?

---

## *MATERIALS NEEDED*

- Long balloons
- Paper bags (somewhat larger than lunch size)
- Masking tape
- Monofilament fishline

- Plastic drinking straw
- Paper
- Pencil

## *PROCEDURE*

1. Inflate a long balloon and release it. On your paper write some words to describe its path of flight.
2. The balloon uses the principle of action-reaction to move. Can you see how it works? Make a picture of an inflated balloon with air coming out. Draw arrows showing the direction of action and reaction.
3. Look at the words you used to describe the path of the balloon's first flight. Try the following to correct the problems.
4. Locate the straw on the fishline stretching across your classroom. Tape a top and bottom corner of the brown paper bag to the straw, parallel with the bag.
5. Slide the bag and straw to the center of the line and put a long, inflated balloon in the open bag.
6. Release the air rapidly from the balloon. What happened?
7. Pretend your paper bag is a rocket ship and the balloon is a powerful rocket engine. What could you do to improve its flight? Test your ideas.

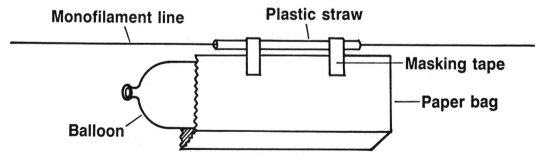

FIGURE 148-1. Brown bag with balloon in it.

## TEACHER INFORMATION

The balloon acts as a simple reaction (rocket) engine. When it is released by itself, its flight will be very erratic or unpredictable.

The monofilament line, straw, and paper bag provide housing, control, and direction for the thrust of the rocket engine. These are three essentials needed for space travel.

While experimenting to obtain greater speed and distance, you might suggest trying different-sized tubes as nozzles for the exhaust end of the rocket. Will a smaller opening (barrel of old ball point pen) make greater distances possible? Should the opening at the end of the balloon be larger (copper pipe)? How can you get both greater speed and greater distance (less mass, larger engine)?

# ACTIVITY 149: How Can We Develop More Thrust?

(Teacher-supervised activity)

## MATERIALS NEEDED

- Empty tube from paper towel or toilet tissue
- Heavy cardboard
- Monofilament line (15-lb. strength)
- $CO_2$ capsules
- Screw eyes

- Scissors
- Iron wire
- Hammer
- Sharpened nail
- Strong glue
- Stapler

## PROCEDURE

1. Cut three tail fins from the heavy cardboard. Glue them lengthwise around one end of the cardboard tube.
2. Make a circle approximately 10 cm (4 in.) in diameter. Cut from one edge into the center and fold it over to make a cone (glue and hold with staples).
3. Glue the nose cone to the end of the tube opposite the fins.
4. Attach two screw eyes or loops of wire to the top of the tube. Secure them with glue.
5. Use cardboard and crossed pieces of iron wire to make a holder for your $CO_2$ capsule. Insert it in the rear of the tube.
6. String monofilament line through the cup eyes.
7. Take your rocket outside and locate two uprights (trees or poles) about 50 meters (50 yards) apart. Stretch the monoline with the rocket attached very tightly between the uprights. Be sure there is nothing else near the line.

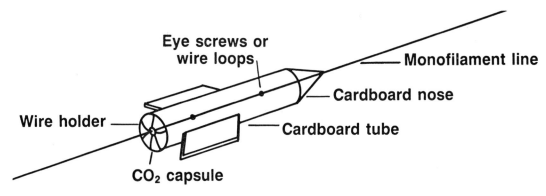

FIGURE 149-1. $CO_2$ rocket on monofilament line.

8.  Have a friend hold the rocket while you use a hammer and sharp nail to punch a small hole in the narrow end of the $CO_2$ capsule. Release the rocket immediately.
9.  Try this several times.

## TEACHER INFORMATION

The $CO_2$ capsule rocket is relatively safe, but close supervision is recommended in case of unexpected events. The sharpened nail and hammer, used to puncture the $CO_2$ capsule are potential hazards if used carelessly.

When properly punctured and released, the rocket will travel down the line at a high rate of speed. The students may have to practice several times to get a successful launch. $CO_2$ capsules can be purchased at sporting goods stores and hobby shops.

Be sure all students remain behind the point of the rocket launch and that there are no obstructions along the path of the line. Use heavy-weight monofilament line (at least 15-pound test) and stretch it as tightly as possible (at least four feet above the ground).

All students can construct and launch rockets safely if the directions are carefully followed. The purchase of $CO_2$ capsules will entail some expense. Check local prices before you begin.

Students may notice that the capsules become very cold after they have been "triggered." This is because of a physical principle concerning gas under pressure: When released it takes on heat energy. This same principle is used to cool refrigerating systems (see the encyclopedia).

## ENRICHMENT IDEA:

Toy stores often sell plastic "water rockets" of one or more stages. They are inexpensive and safe but must be used outdoors. These rockets are exciting to watch and demonstrate the action-reaction principle very well.

# ACTIVITY 150: How Do Other Forces Affect Our Rocket's Performance?

## MATERIALS NEEDED

- Long balloon
- Plastic drinking straw
- Monofilament line
- Masking tape

## PROCEDURE

1. Thread the monofilament line through the straw and attach it, tightly stretched, to opposite sides of your classroom.
2. Inflate a long balloon. Hold its mouth closed while using masking tape to secure it to the straw.
3. Release the balloon. What happened?
4. Compare the performance of this balloon to that of the balloon in the paper bag in Activity 148. Can you think of reasons for the differences you observed?

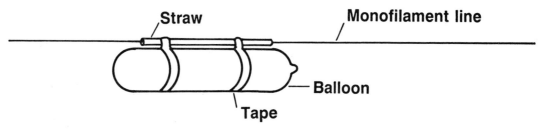

FIGURE 150-1. Balloon on monofilament line.

## TEACHER INFORMATION

Without the paper bag, the balloon will move down the line at a higher rate of speed for a greater distance. Children may decide that the "weight" of the bag reduced the performance. Others may suggest that the square shape of the bag slowed it down. Some may notice that the balloon without the bag seems to get a faster start. These observations are related to the forces that are acting upon the object: gravity, inertia, and friction (wind resistance). If we are to travel into outer space, all three must be considered.

# ACTIVITY 151: How Does Gravity Affect Objects?

## MATERIALS NEEDED

- Objects of different sizes and weights (ping-pong ball, tennis ball, golf ball, marble, rock, large Styrofoam ball, and so on)

- Meter stick, yardstick, or long board

## PROCEDURE

1. Place several of the objects close together on the edge of a flat table.
2. Find several students to be observers.
3. Use the long stick to push all the objects off the table at the same time (a rapid, even push is better than a slow, gradual one).
4. Have your observers report which object hit the floor first.
5. Try several times until you are certain of the results.
6. Find a shelf or ledge to launch the objects from a greater height. What do your observers report?

## TEACHER INFORMATION

If wind resistance (air friction) does not affect them, all objects fall at the same rate. Therefore, if dropped at the same instant and from the same height, they will hit the ground at the same time. The rate of fall does not depend on the size or weight of an object. This is a very difficult concept for children (and many adults) to understand. Our logic seems to say "Big, heavy rocks will fall faster than tiny pebbles." The story is told of Galileo's dropping large and small objects at the same time from the Leaning Tower of Pisa centuries ago. This was the principle he discovered: Shapes and mass do not affect the rate of fall.

# ACTIVITY 152:  How Does Inertia Affect Objects

(Teacher-supervised activity)

## *MATERIALS NEEDED*

- Plastic tumbler half full of water
- Meter stick or yardstick

- Four or five blocks 10 cm. × 10 cm. (4 in. × 4 in.) cut from a two-by-four plank

## *PROCEDURE*

1. Before you begin, review Activities 16 and 17 in Section 1, "Starter Ideas." If you have not done them yet, do them now.
2. Stack the square blocks on a flat, smooth surface (table). Be sure no one is around you.
3. Rest your meter stick on the table behind the stack of blocks.
4. Hold the meter stick at one end and strike the bottom block with a smooth, rapid, sliding movement.
5. Repeat step 4 as many times as you can.
6. Stack the blocks again. Put a plastic tumbler half full of water on the top block.
7. Can you make the glass with the water stand on the table without touching it or spilling any of the water?

## *TEACHER INFORMATION*

Be sure this investigation is done in an area where neither flying blocks nor spilled water will cause damage.

The blocks should be sanded so they are smooth and then polished to reduce friction.

As they strike the blocks, students may need to practice in developing a smooth, gliding motion with follow-through as they would in baseball, golf, or tennis. With practice, the blocks can be removed one at a time. The plastic tumbler should behave as the other blocks do.

Newton's law states that objects in motion remain in motion and objects at rest remain at rest unless acted upon by an outside force. If you try to stop a moving object (catch a ball) or move a stationary object (the block), its resistance to change is called *inertia*. By using smooth blocks to reduce the friction, we can move a single block without disturbing the others because the inertia of the other blocks will be greater than the friction. If you're tempted to leave the plastic tumbler empty, remember, the greater the mass, the more inertia it has. An empty tumbler is more likely to topple than a full one. A short, squat tumbler will be more stable than a tall, narrow one.

# ACTIVITY 153: How Do Gravity and Inertia Affect Space Travel?

## MATERIALS NEEDED

- Blocks used in Activity 152
- Paper
- Pencil

## PROCEDURE

1. Stack one block on top of another. Pretend the bottom block is an automobile and the top block is the passenger. Touching the automobile part only, move it and the passenger across the table and make it crash head-on into another block. What happened? In most automobiles, there are devices designed to protect passengers in a situation like this. Can you name them? Draw the block and use arrows to show what happened.

2. Put the passenger block on top of the automobile block again. Without touching them, use a third block to crash into the rear of the stationary automobile block. What happened? Can you think of devices in most automobiles designed to protect passengers in this situation? Draw the blocks and use arrows to show what happened to the passenger.

3. Use your understanding of inertia to explain what would happen if these crashes occurred in space without safety devices. Since there is no gravity or friction in space, what would happen to the passenger? Draw the blocks and use arrows to show what happens to them.

## TEACHER INFORMATION

This activity should help students relate inertia to familiar situations. Step 1 illustrates the importance of using seatbelts. The arrows in the first drawing should show the top block continuing forward (inertia) after the "head-on" crash and then falling to the ground (gravity). The arrows in the rear-end collision in step 2 should show the block continuing on with the passenger remaining stationary. Since the passengers cannot remain stationary in a real car, they are thrown back against the seat and unless their heads are protected by a headrest (safety device) they receive a painful and often serious neck injury called *whiplash*.

In the third step, several possibilities could occur. In a head-on crash the passenger might be thrown forward out of the automobile and, since neither gravity nor friction would stop the forward-motion, continue on in a straight line forever. If a rear-end crash occurred and the passengers were not thrown out, they would be pushed against the seats with the same force as they were on earth. If the passengers were thrown out of the automobile, it would continue on in a straight line and the passengers would be left weightless and stationary in space (no gravity to cause them to fall).

# ACTIVITY 154:  Have You Ever Felt Weightless?

(Small-group activity)

## *MATERIALS NEEDED*

- Clear plastic drinking glass
- Clear plastic sandwich bag
- Hard-boiled egg
- Spring scale
- Salt

- Tablespoon
- String 20 cm. (8 in.) long
- Warm water
- Paper
- Pencil

## *PROCEDURE*

1. Peel the hard-boiled egg and put it in the plastic bag.
2. Attach a 20-cm. piece of string to the spring scale. Attach the other end to the plastic bag, being sure no air is trapped in the bag. Record the weight of the egg.
3. While it is still attached to the string and scale, lower the egg into a glass two-thirds full of warm water.
4. While the egg is submerged in the water but not touching the bottom, record its weigh again.
5. Lower the egg to the bottom of the glass while it is still attached to the string and scale, but don't support its weight.
6. Add salt, one tablespoon at a time, until the egg begins to move off the bottom of the glass.
7. Check and record its weight again.
8. Compare your first and last record of the egg's weight.
9. If you have ever gone deep in the water while swimming, you may have felt like the egg. As the density of the medium (substance) in which the egg is placed increases from air, to water, to salt water, the egg will appear to weight less. In a swimming pool, the water pressure, as you go deeper, creates the same effect, and at a certain depth you feel weightless. You may have felt this same sensation at an amusement park if you took a ride that lifted you off the seat. Astronauts are trained to move around in a weightless environment by spending time experiencing weightlessness in a deep pool. Discuss this with your teacher and other members of your class.

## *TEACHER INFORMATION*

Although weightlessness as a result of density and water pressure has different causes, the observed behavior is the same. The egg demonstration will show students that the weight of an object, as measured by a scale, is relative and can be changed in several ways. As you speed over the top to begin the second dip on a roller coaster or similar ride, inertia, the tendency of your body to continue upward, creates the same weightless feeling again for a different reason. The pull of gravity decreases rapidly as an object moves away from the earth's surface. Anyone who has flown more than 50 miles above the earth's surface is a space traveler, or an astronaut.

NASA films of all space flights are available. Check with your local library.

*Section 8*

---

# *BEYOND THE EARTH*

# TO THE TEACHER

Although they are observable at a distance, much information about our neighboring planets, moon, and other satellites is yet to be discovered. The rapid explosion of new technology has produced an overwhelming amount of new information to astronomers. As you read this page, hundreds of satellites and controlled space vehicles are beaming messages, pictures, and other information about our neighbors in space. At the same time, other satellites are studying the earth and communicating new information about the weather, topography, temperature, and other features of our home planet. Astronomy and the resultant technology are on the growing edge of scientific knowledge.

Many of the numbers, distances, temperatures, and figures that we learn today will change tomorrow. If you ask students the number of planets and they say eight or ten instead of the traditional nine, think before marking them wrong. By many criteria, Jupiter can be classified as a sun and many astronomers believe there are planets beyond Pluto in our solar system.

And what of intelligent life in the universe? Many astronomers believe it is just a matter of time until we are in contact. Time is related to speed, distance, and space in ways few of us can even comprehend.

In this rapidly changing field of knowledge, be wary of teaching facts as absolute. Much information is tentative and changing.

As they begin to sense the incredible order and grandeur of the universe, your students will stand in awe and wonder. We invite you to direct the following activities toward that goal.

*National Geographic* (December 1969) produced exceptionally fine coverage and photographs of the first manned moon landing and exploration. Included was a small phonograph record narrated by astronaut Frank Borman, telling of the Apollo flights that led to the magnificent achievement. Neil Armstrong's first words as he stepped on the moon are recorded. This particular issue of *National Geographic* is strongly recommended, especially for students in grades 4-8. Check with your media center or public library.

# ACTIVITY 155: What Does Our Earth Look Like?

(Partners and total-group activity)

## MATERIALS NEEDED

- Globe of the earth
- Pencil
- Newsprint

- Color photographs of the earth taken from the moon

## PROCEDURE

1. Pretend you are an astronaut and have just landed on the moon. You are on the side facing the earth. Choose a friend and describe how the earth looks from your position. Have your friend record words that tell what you think you would see.
2. Examine the globe in your classroom. It is a ball-shaped map of the earth. Can you think of any ways your view from the moon might be different from your classroom view of the globe?
3. Your teacher has actual photographs of the earth that were taken by astronauts from the moon. Discuss with your teacher and the rest of the class ways the globe is like and unlike photos of the earth.

## TEACHER INFORMATION

This introductory activity may be omitted if students are already familiar with photographs of the earth taken from space. The purpose of this activity is to introduce the globe as a fairly accurate model of the earth's surface.

In photos, clouds will often cover large portions of the earth's surface. Complete storm systems are often visible. Contrasting colors of land and water can be seen clearly. The atmosphere around the earth cannot be seen except where clouds are present. The blue sky we see from the surface of the earth is due to scattering and absorption of different wavelengths of light as the sun's light travels through the earth's atmosphere.

Photographs of the earth taken from the moon are available in encyclopedias, periodicals (especially *National Geographic*), library books after 1969, and probably your school media center.

232 Beyond the Earth

# ACTIVITY 156: How Does the Earth Move?

(Total-group activity)

## MATERIALS NEEDED

- Large playground ball
- Axis-mounted globe of the earth
- Small pieces of gummed paper

## PROCEDURE

1. Today we are going to begin the construction of a model of the sun and some of the large objects in orbit around it. Place the playground ball on a table near the center of the room.
2. Observe the globe. Notice it is attached to the mount at two points. These are the ends of an imaginary line running through the center of the earth, called the *axis*. We call these two points the *North* and *South Poles*.
3. Make the playground ball spin. As it spins, can you find the axis (point around which it spins)? What happens when it begins to slow down? Can you think of reasons why it slows down?
4. Spin the globe. Is its movement different from that of the ball? Explain.
5. The turning of the earth on its axis is called *rotation*. It turns completely around once in every 24 hours.
6. Use the globe to locate the place where you live. Put a small gummed paper on that spot.
7. Put the globe in a corner of the room and pretend you are standing on the paper trying to see the playground ball (sun) in the center of the room.
8. Slowly rotate (turn) the globe completely around. If you are standing on the globe and it is rotating, how much of the time will you be able to see the sun (playground ball)? Can you see what makes night and day where you live?

## TEACHER INFORMATION

The concept that the earth rotates on its axis may seem simple to the adult mind, but it is extremely important to the whole idea of solar movement and change in our solar system and the universe. If we rely on past experience of movement and our powers of observation, simple logic may convince us that the earth stands still and the sun moves around it. For centuries some influential philosophers and astrologers in the Western world held this belief (See "Ptolemaic Theory" in the encyclopedia). In the sixteenth century, Copernicus, Kepler, and Galileo discovered the correct principles of solar movement. As enrichment, older students may be interested in studying the history of these discoveries (see Activity 158).

At the equator the earth rotates at a speed of approximately 1,000 miles per hour. We do not sense any movement because everything, including our atmosphere, is moving at a smooth pace. On the earth we have learned to judge speed by the rush of wind, vibration, sound, abrupt changes in gravity and speed (inertia), and the rate at which we pass reference points, such as fence posts. In space, with the exception of inertia, none of the usual phenomena associated with movement are present. For this reason, astronauts traveling in orbit around the earth at over 17,000 miles an hour feel no sensation of movement. From the moon, the earth would not appear to be rotating. It would take several hours of observation to detect movement. You should be aware that the exact rotation time of the earth is a fraction less than 24 hours. Scientists correct for this by occasionally adding one second to the official worldwide standard time kept in Greenwich, England.

The next activity develops the concepts of the earth's revolution around the sun and why seasons occur.

# ACTIVITY 157:  How Does the Earth Travel?

(Total-group activity)

## *MATERIALS NEEDED*

- Axis-mounted globe of the earth
- Large playground ball
- One copy of Figure 157-1 for each student

## *PROCEDURE*

1. In addition to *rotating* on its axis once very 24 hours, the earth also *revolves* or travels around the sun, once a year (365¼ days). Hold the globe in your hand and spin it evenly (not too fast) while you walk completely around the playground ball. You have now performed the basic movements the earth and other planets make in the solar system. It took thousands of years for people to make this basic discovery.

2. The earth is kept in the same path around the sun because of the attraction of the sun's gravity. The path an object follows as it revolves around another object is called an *orbit*. Study the drawing your teacher has given you. During a yearly trip around the sun, the earth is shown in four positions in its *orbit*. Notice that the earth travels in a *counterclockwise* direction.

3. Observe the globe and the diagram of the Earth revolving around the sun. Notice that the axis upon which the earth rotates is not upright but tilted approximately 23.5°. As it revolves around the sun, the north end of the earth's axis continues to point toward a relatively stationary object in the sky called the North Star. Notice in the diagram that the axis in all four drawings of the earth would come together (converge) at a distant point if you continued to draw them in a straight line. This would be the location of the North Star.

4. The North and South American continents are shown on all four diagrams of the earth. Observe that the unchanging tilt of the earth causes the North American continent to tilt toward and away from the direct rays of the sun in its annual progress. When the continent is tipped toward the sun, the more direct rays produce more heat and cause summer. Tilting away from the direct rays causes winter. Twice a year the angle of the rays is equal. These are the times of the *vernal equinox* (spring) and the *autumnal equinox* (autumn, or fall). Winter and summer come at opposite ends of the earth's orbit and are called summer and winter *solstice*.

## *TEACHER INFORMATION*

Most students will be able to understand the simple solar mechanics of rotation and revolution (steps 1 and 2).

The tilt of the earth and its effect on seasonal change requires abstract visualization and formal thinking, for which many elementary students may not be developmentally ready. The diagram may help concrete thinkers to visualize seasonal change, but many may continue to believe that the earth is closer to the sun in the summer and farther away in winter, although the opposite is true in our hemisphere. This activity has been divided into two parts, steps 1 and 2 and steps 3 and 4. Later activities will *not* depend on concepts developed in steps 3 and 4.

## A NOTE TO TEACHERS OF YOUNG CHILDREN

A method of teaching the simple ideas of rotation and revolution can be developed through role playing. Have one child be the sun and stand in the center of the room. Have another be the earth and slowly walk (revolve) around the "sun" while turning around (rotation) at the same time. Point out that in order to be accurate, the "earth" child would need to turn around (rotate) three hundred sixty-five and one-fourth (365¼) times each trip around the sun.

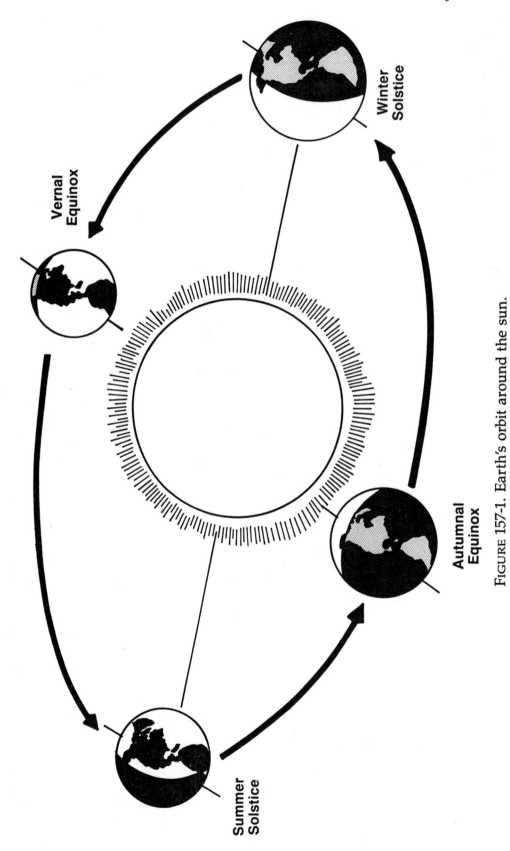

FIGURE 157-1. Earth's orbit around the sun.

# ACTIVITY 158: What Paths Do Earth and Similar Objects Follow?

(Individual and small-group activity)

## MATERIALS NEEDED

- Rubber ball attached to elastic 1 m. (1 yd.) long (or paddleball toy)
- 8- or 12-ounce Styrofoam cup
- 45-cm. × 45 cm. (18 in. × 18 in.) or larger cardboard box for base
- 45-cm × 45 cm. (18 in. × 18 in.) unlined white paper

- String 20 cm. (8 in.) long
- String 60 cm. (24 in.) long
- Thumbtacks or pushpins
- Sharp pencil
- Colored pencils

## PROCEDURE

1. Before the sixteenth century most people in the Western world (Europe) believed the earth stood still and the sun, moon, and stars all revolved around it. Copernicus was the first man to state the idea that the sun was in the center of a system and that the earth and some other bodies revolved around it. The path of the earth around the sun was called an *orbit.* Place your paper on the cardboard box. In the center of your paper make a picture of the sun.
2. Using a thumbtack, attach one end of the 20-cm. (8-in.) length of string to the center of your picture of the sun. Tie your pencil to the other end of the string.
3. Keeping the string *taut* at all times, use the point of your pencil to draw a circle around the sun on the paper. Draw a picture of the earth on the circle. This model is similar to the idea Copernicus had of the earth's path around the sun. A few stars, called *planets* (Greek word meaning "wandering star"), also moved through the sky in strange ways. Copernicus believed these "stars" were bodies similar to earth and also moved in circles around the sun.
4. Soon after Copernicus made his ideas known, a mathematician named Johannes Kepler observed that the actual movement of the earth and other planets did not quite agree with Copernicus' theory. Using his mathematical knowledge, Kepler changed the round paths or orbits to slightly *elongated* orbits called *ellipses.* There are several ways you can draw an ellipse. One of the easiest is to use the mouth of a Styrofoam cup. Put the cup, mouth down on a piece of paper. With your pencil, move the point around the mouth to make a circle. Now hold the cup in its center with your thumb on one side and your fingers on the other. Gently squeeze until the mouth of the cup is no longer round. With your pencil trace the mouth. Can you see how a circle can be elongated to form an ellipse?

5. If you have ever played with a small ball attached to an elastic, you have probably accidentally or on purpose made an ellipse. Hold the end of the elastic or paddle so the ball nearly touches the floor. Slowly move your hand or the paddle around and around until the ball is moving in a circular path. Now, gradually change the motion of your hand so it moves back and forth rather than in a circle. Observe the path of the ball. Describe the changes you see.

6. You can draw an ellipse over the first picture model of the sun and earth you drew on the large piece of paper (steps 2 and 3 above). Tie the ends of the 60-cm. (24-in.) string together. Press two thumbtacks halfway into the paper and cardboard box 20 cm. (8 in.) apart in a line across the picture of the sun. Place the circular string loosely under the two thumbtacks. With your pencil, stretch the string taut under the thumbtacks. Keep the string taut but allow it to make a circle. What happened? Can you change the shape of your ellipse by moving one thumbtack? What happens if you move both thumbtacks? Kepler discovered that the planets in our *solar* (sun) *system* move in paths that are slightly elliptical. In later times, other members of our solar system, such as some comets, were found to have very elongated elliptical orbits.

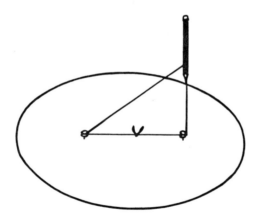

FIGURE 158-1. Apparatus for making an orbit.

## TEACHER INFORMATION

The theory of Copernicus, modified by Kepler and later verified by Galileo, did not electrify the scientific community in the seventeenth century. Galileo was convicted of heresy, partly because of his strong support of the Copernican model of the solar system. The purpose of this activity is to emphasize that objects in the solar system travel in elliptical, and not round, orbits as are often pictured. You may be able to communicate this concept by using one or two, rather than all, of the activities. It is important for students to understand that orbital paths vary. The paths of the two outermost known planets, Neptune and Pluto, cross each other. Halley's Comet, which passed Earth in 1985 and 1986, is in a greatly elongated orbit that carries it beyond Pluto during its 75-year journey.

# ACTIVITY 159: How Do Man-Made Satellites Help Us?

(Total-group activity)

## MATERIALS NEEDED

- Globe of the earth
- 1-cm. (¼-in.) ball of aluminum foil
- Bits of gummed paper
- Pencil

## PROCEDURE

1. Attach a small piece of gummed paper on the globe and mark the spot where you live and, with the point of your pencil, make a tiny dot on the paper. If your globe is an average size, 30–40 cm. (12–16 in.), you, your school, and your community could fit within the tiny dot on the paper. In fact, the dot represents the greatest portion of the earth's surface that can be seen fron any given location on the earth. Can you think of ways to help you see a greater distance?

2. Since television and some other communication signals travel in a straight line, they can travel only short distances without being relayed (passed on) in some way. Hold an aluminum foil ball above the spot you marked on your globe. Have someone slowly turn the globe while you keep the foil ball directly above the mark. Notice that the foil ball is moving at a speed that matches the rotation of the earth. This is the way communication satellites work. If you were very small, standing at the marked point, would the foil ball appear to be moving? Why? Look at Figure 159-1. With the ball acting as a reflector, television signals could be sent to you from a great distance away, in the same way that a mirror reflects light.

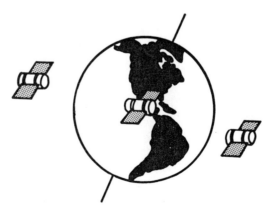

FIGURE 159-1. Earth with communication satellites in orbit.

3.  Look at Figure 159-2. The orbit of this satellite is elliptical. At one point, the satellite comes very near the earth. This is called the *perigee*. The greatest distance a satellite moves away from a parent body is called the *apogee*. Scientists often put satellites in elliptical orbits to study a specific area of the earth or sky.

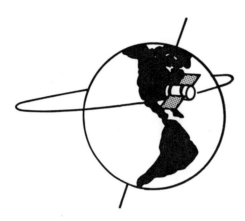

FIGURE 159-2. Earth with satellite in sharp ellipse.

## TEACHER INFORMATION

Although the foil ball is too large to be to scale either in size or distance, from the point marked on the globe by the students, it would appear to be stationary. To be in scale it would need to be of microscopic size.

Orbits of satellites launched in space by NASA (National Aeronautics and Space Administration) vary according to the purpose of the satellite. Some are in "stationary" orbits that are almost round and almost exactly match the speed of the earth's rotation. These communication satellites appear to "hang" stationary in the sky and reflect and relay television signals around the earth. Telecommunications for the entire world depend on these satellites (see Figure 159-1). Some satellites are put in greatly elongated orbits in order to come very near the earth at a specific point. Satellites are also used to relay weather information, specific geographic data (including geothermal and faulting), and for military purposes.

In an elliptical orbit, the point at which a satellite is closest to its parent body is called the *perigee*. The point furthest from the parent body is called the *apogee* (Figure 159-2). There have been thousands of man-made satellites launched in orbit around the earth during the past three decades, 1957 to the present. Many of them are no longer useful. See the encyclopedia and specific library books for further information.

# ACTIVITY 160: How Is Our Moon a Natural Satellite?

(Total-group activity)

## MATERIALS NEEDED

- Pencil
- Paper

- One copy of "Do You Know This about the Moon?" for each student

## PROCEDURE

1. Everyone in your class knows something about the moon. Meet in groups of four or five students each and record everything your group knows about the moon and what it does.
2. Come together as a whole group and take turns sharing your information about the moon. Have someone record all the information on the chalkboard.
3. Use the information on the chalkboard to answer the "Do You Know This About the Moon?" activity sheet.
4. If you do not have enough information to answer all the questions, save the activity sheet to use as you do Activities 161 and 162.

## TEACHER INFORMATION

The activity sheet is intended for motivation only and should not be used for evaluation.

With the exception of the earth, scientists know more about the moon than any other object in the solar system or the universe. Your students may be familiar with many scientific facts about the moon, yet not fully understand the basic motions of the earth and the moon and their relationships to the sun. The purpose of the following activities is to establish a concept of the relationships involved as objects move in a solar system. More detailed answers to the activity sheet may be found in your encyclopedia. Tides (Question 9) are not developed in these activities. If students can observe or experience tides in your region of the country, see your encyclopedia or library books for specific activities and information.

## ANSWERS TO "DO YOU KNOW THIS ABOUT THE MOON?"

1. The moon has a diameter of nearly 2,500 miles, roughly the same distance as from coast to coast on the Continental United States.
2. 225,745 miles
3. 28 days
4. Yes, once for each revolution.

5. Apparent changes in shape of the moon.
6. Amount of reflected light depending on the position of the moon in relation to the earth and the sun.
7. Earth rotates more rapidly than the moon revolves around it.
8. Dark material on the surface. Probably ancient volcanic flows.
9. Causes tides, possibly some earthquakes.
10. 10 pounds. The pull of the moon's gravity is one sixth (⅙) that of the earth.

Name _____ Date _____

# Do You Know This About the Moon?

1. How large is the moon compared with the earth? _____

   _____

2. What is the average distance from Earth to the moon? _____

   _____

3. How long does it take the moon to revolve around the earth? _____

   _____

4. Since the moon always keeps the same side facing Earth, does it rotate on its own axis?

   _____

5. What are phases of the moon? _____

   _____

6. What causes phases of the moon? _____

   _____

7. Why is the moon often visible in the daytime? _____

   _____

8. What causes the "man in the moon"? _____

   _____

9. How does the moon's gravity affect Earth? _____

   _____

10 If you weigh 60 pounds on Earth, how much would you weigh on the moon?

   _____

# ACTIVITY 161: How Does the Moon Travel Around the Earth?

(Total-group activity)

## MATERIALS NEEDED

- Globe of earth
- Large Styrofoam ball with one half painted black
- Round toothpick
- Small piece of gummed paper

## PROCEDURE

1. Locate on the globe the place where you live and put a tiny piece of gummed paper on that spot.
2. The black and white Styrofoam ball represents our moon. The moon revolves around the earth once in approximately 28 days. The same side of the moon (in this case the lighter side) always faces the earth. Have another student hold the moon and walk slowly around the earth (globe) while keeping the light side facing it.
3. Rotate the globe 28 times while the moon goes around it once.
4. As the moon goes around the earth, pretend you are standing on the tiny bit of paper. Notice that part of the time you would not be able to see the moon.
5. From the model, you can easily see that you and the earth rotate and that the moon revolves. Does the moon also rotate? Stick a round toothpick through the Styrofoam ball where the white and black halves meet. The toothpick now represents the moon's axis. Hold the toothpick firmly and walk around the globe. What happens to the light side of the moon? What must you do to keep the motions of the earth and moon in correct relationship? What can you say about the rotation of the moon?

## TEACHER INFORMATION

The moon rotates once each time it revolves, thereby always keeping the same side facing the earth. When the toothpick is held firmly, the dark side becomes visible from the earth during the moon's revolution. The moon must rotate once each time it revolves. When the model of the moon is held by a toothpick, it must be manually rotated to keep the light side facing the earth.

To give some idea of scale, the ideal-sized Styrofoam ball should have approximately the same diameter as the distance across the United States on your globe (scale size is not essential to this activity).

# ACTIVITY 162: What Is the Appearance of the Surface of the Moon?

(Small-group, teacher-directed activity in darkened room)

- One large Styrofoam ball
- Magnifying glass
- Brown poster paint

- Lamp with exposed light bulb
- Meter stick (yardstick), large screwdriver, or similar dull objects

## PROCEDURE

1. In a darkened room, bring a Styrofoam ball to within one meter of the light bulb. Use the magnifying glass to examine the surface of the Styrofoam ball (globe). Under magnification you will notice that the surface is rough and has many dents in it. Notice that the indentations cast tiny shadows. The surface of your Styrofoam ball is similar to the moon's surface except the moon has more irregularities. Scientists believe the craters or dents and mountains on the moon were caused by volcanic flows (dark color) and countless numbers of collisions with large solid objects from space, mostly *meteors.*

2. Carefully use the end of a meter stick, a large screwdriver, or a similar dull object to make several additional meteor "strikes" on the moon model. (Remember, most meteors will not come straight in but will strike from different angles.) Pour brown paint (representing lava) in some of the craters.

3. Place your Styrofoam ball near the light again. Observe it from two or three meters (yards) away. Can you see why there appears to be "a man in the moon"?

## TEACHER INFORMATION

The friction caused by the atmosphere of our earth protects us from most small meteors, usually causing them to burn up before reaching the ground. Large meteors have struck the earth in the past and will probably do so in the future. Many scientists believe that most large species of dinosaurs were killed within a short span of time by dust caused when a large meteor strike blocked the sun for several months (or years) and killed most of the vegetation upon which the dinosaurs depended for food.

Many scientists believe that the moon once had a hot liquid core but as it cooled, volcanic activity ceased and molten materials no longer flowed on the surface. Plate tectonics (see Activity 90) also ceased and the moon's surface has become increasingly scarred by meteor damage (estimated time: 3 to 4½ billion years; very heavy meteor bombardment in early years, followed by massive dark lava flows before cooling).

*Note:* The material here is intended as teacher background information only. It is not necessarily recommended as content suitable for elementary-age students.

# ACTIVITY 163: What Are Phases of the Moon?

(Teacher-supervised activity)

## *MATERIALS NEEDED*

- Oil lamp
- Match
- Large Styrofoam ball
- Meter stick or yardstick
- String 50 cm. (20 in.) long

- Masking tape
- Pencil
- Paper
- Chair

## *PROCEDURE*

1. Tape one end of the string to the Styrofoam ball and the other end to the meter stick.
2. Have your partner sit on a chair. Stand behind your partner and hold the meter stick horizontally at arm's length so the Styrofoam ball is hanging in front of your partner at about his or her eye level.
3. Slowly move the meter stick in a counterclockwise direction. Have your partner turn in the chair and observe the ball (moon) while it makes a complete circle. This is the way the moon would appear to you on earth if light came from all directions or if the moon produced its own light, as the sun does.
4. Place the oil lamp on a chair approximately 2 meters (2 yards) behind and to the right of your partner.
5. Carefully light the oil lamp and replace the chimney.
6. Darken the room. Move the ball around on the meter stick until your partner says it appears brightest. This position should be almost directly opposite the light source.
7. Slowly move the ball one-fourth of a revolution, similar to the movement you made in step 3. Stop. Observe the ball carefully. How much is now brightly lighted? Which side(s)?
8. Continue to move the ball slowly in one complete revolution. Stop and carefully observe at intervals of one-fourth of a revolution.
9. Trade places with your partner and perform a second revolution. Draw four circles on a sheet of paper and use your pencil to shade the circles so they resemble the ones you observe.
10. Try stopping between each of the original four stops, and draw four additional circles, one between each of the original four. Shade them to show what you see.
11. After everyone has completed the activity, discuss it and compare your diagrams with those of the rest of your group.
12. Review Activity 19 in Section 1, "Starter Ideas."

FIGURE 163-1. Partners showing the phases of the moon.

## TEACHER INFORMATION

Phases of the moon are difficult to portray in a realistic manner. In most schools, it is impossible to find a completely dark room where no light is reflected. The oil lamp will provide a soft light with less reflected glare. However, under almost all conditions, the students will be able to see the part of the ball that is in shadow. Students should understand that only the bright part of the ball represents the light the moon reflects.

The eight common phases of the moon are shown in Figure 163-2.

If shadows interfere as the ball representing the moon is revolved around the student sitting on the chair, try elevating the ball.

*Note:* If an oil lamp is not available or there is concern about safety, use a 15-watt electric light bulb instead.

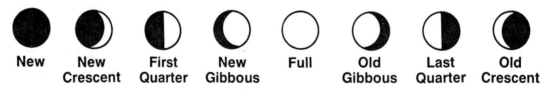

| New | New Crescent | First Quarter | New Gibbous | Full | Old Gibbous | Last Quarter | Old Crescent |

FIGURE 163-2. The eight phases of the moon.

# ACTIVITY 164:  What Is an Eclipse?

(Partners in darkened room)

## *MATERIALS NEEDED*

- Large Styrofoam ball with 10–15 cm. (4–6 in.) diameter
- Small Styrofoam ball with 3– cm. (1–2 in.) diameter
- Coat-hanger wire 15 cm. (6 in.) long
- Two pieces of coat-hanger wire 5 cm. (2 in.) long
- Flashlight

## *PROCEDURE*

1. Use the longer wire to attach the two Styrofoam balls together. The larger ball represents the earth. The smaller ball represents the moon.
2. Attach the two smaller pieces of wire to the large ball, one at the top and one at the bottom about where the North and South Poles would be located.
3. Darken the room and hold a flashlight about one meter (1 yard) from the larger ball. The light represents the sun.
4. Hold the large Styrofoam ball by the wires representing the poles and slowly rotate it in a counterclockwise direction. As the moon passes between the sun and the earth, notice what happens. What can you say about this? How much of the large ball is affected?
5. Continue turning the earth until it comes between the moon and the light. How much of the smaller ball was darkened?
6. Pretend you are standing on the earth at a spot where both steps 4 and 5 happened. In step 4 you would be observing a *solar eclipse*. Eclipses of the sun (where the moon is in a position to block out the light from the sun) are quite rare. A *total eclipse*, when the moon completely blocks the sun, will occur on small areas of the earth. When this happens, scientists gather from throughout the world to study the *corona* or bright halo around the sun.

**PLEASE REMEMBER. It is extremely dangerous to look at the sun with the naked eye or even very dark glasses. Eye damage or blindness may occur.**

In step 5 from the earth you would be observing a *lunar eclipse* (when the Earth blocks the moon's reflected light). Partially because the moon is much smaller, lunar eclipses (when you see the earth's shadow covering the moon) are much more common.

## *TEACHER INFORMATION*

Solar eclipses, even partial, occur rarely on any single area of the earth. Media will inform you well in advance when a solar eclipse is to occur. *Never* look at the sun. Contact a high school or college physics department for suggestions for viewing the eclipse with reflected light. Observing lunar eclipses will not harm the eyes. However, since they usually occur at night, they may be damaging to your sleep patterns!

# ACTIVITY 165: What Is a Solar System?

## *MATERIALS NEEDED*

- One copy of Figure 165-1 for each student
- Paper
- Pencil

## *PROCEDURE*

1. Look at the drawing. This is a picture of our sun and some of the objects that move around it. The strong gravitational attraction of the sun and the weaker pull of the smaller objects keep them in orbit around the sun.
2. Count the planets shown in the diagram. Scientists have identified nine planets and a ring of millions of solid particles called the *asteroid belt*.
3. On your paper write the names of the four planets closest to the sun. These are sometimes called the *rocky* planets because they are made of solid materials. The earth is a rocky planet.
4. Write the names of the next two planets. These are sometimes called the giant planets. They are very large and in many ways like the sun.
5. Write the names of the last three planets. These are often called the icy planets because they are so far from the sun their temperatures are very, very cold. Some scientists believe there are other planets even farther out in the solar system. Perhaps, as you are reading this material, another planet may be discovered!

## *TEACHER INFORMATION*

The diagram of the solar system is not presented in scale, either in size or distance. Because of the immense contrast in size and distance, Activities 167 and 168 suggest some ways to portray these differences.

As is shown in the diagram, the orbits of most planets are on a similar plane in relation to the sun. The orbit of Pluto is at a different angle. Scientists have several theories to account for this phenomenon. Your encyclopedia is a good reference source if students are interested.

No attempt has been made to mention or name the many moons or rings in orbit around the planets. Within the past ten years, the number of planets with rings and the number of known moons has almost doubled. The best sources for current teaching information are journals such as the *National Geographic*.

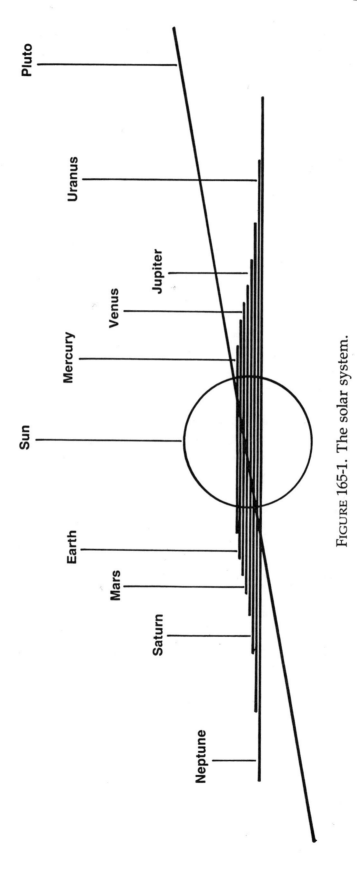

FIGURE 165-1. The solar system.

# ACTIVITY 166: How Can You Study a Planet?

(Groups of five or six students)

## *MATERIALS NEEDED*

- Library books, magazines, encyclopedias, newspaper articles
- Pencil
- Paper

## *PROCEDURE*

1.  New discoveries are being made every day. Much of the information we read about our solar system and other bodies in the sky is increasing rapidly. Choose a planet you would like to study and join other students to form a group.
2.  Use the books and other reference materials to find out as much as you can about your planet. The following may help you begin your study:
    a. Where did your planet get its name?
    b. How was it discovered?
    c. How big is it?
    d. How far is it from the sun?
    e. How long is a day on your planet? How long is a year?
    f. What is the average temperature on your planet?
    g. Do you think you could live on your planet? Why or why not?
    h. Pretend you are on a spaceship flying near your planet. Draw a picture of what you see.
    i. Tell why your planet is special and not like any others.
3.  Plan a way to share your findings with the rest of the class.

## *TEACHER INFORMATION*

The earth should not be included in the planets studied. Knowledge of the earth will increase, since it is used as a base or standard with which other planets are compared. Not all planets need to be studied in depth.

Major goals of the activity will be met if students gain some idea of the vast differences found among the planets and the growing and changing nature of the information we have about them. It is *not* recommended that students be required to memorize factual information about the solar system or the universe. Very general concepts that lead to some understanding of the awesome nature of the universe should be the goal. Remember, if you were one of the unfortunate persons forced to memorize facts about astronomy, much of what you learned is now hopelessly out of date. The January 1985 *National Geographic* is an excellent recent source of current information on the known planets.

# ACTIVITY 167: How Big Is the Solar System?

(Group activity)

## MATERIALS NEEDED

- Basketball
- Two grains of sand

## PROCEDURE

1.  The pictures and diagrams you have been using do not show the real sizes and distances in the solar system. It is difficult to construct a scale model that will fit in your classroom. First, pretend the basketball is the sun. Compare it with a grain of sand. If you pretend the grain of sand is the earth, the earth and sun are in approximate scale to each other. About one million earths could fit inside the sun.
2.  Put the basketball in the center of the room. Measure 3½ meters (almost 4 yards) from the ball and place the grain of sand at that point. The sun (represented by the basketball) and the earth (represented by the grain of sand) are now in approximate scale, both in size and distance.
3.  Pluto in this scale model would be another grain of sand less than half the size of Earth, but you would not be able to see it without a very strong telescope because it would be nearly 100 meters (about 100 yards) away from the sun (basketball).
4.  Think of a football field. It is measured in yards. The field is 100 yards long with white lines running across it at five-yard intervals. Roughly, if you put the basketball (sun) on one goal line, the grain of sand (earth) would be located on the near five-yard line. Pluto, the smaller grain of sand, would be located on the far goal line 100 yards away.

## TEACHER INFORMATION

The scale measurements used in this activity are broad estimates. The differences in size and distance are almost incomprehensible for most young people and adults. Concrete activities such as this and the one following may help to give at least a tiny glimpse of the vastness of our solar system and universe.

# ACTIVITY 168: How Can You Make a Distance Scale Solar System in Your School?

(Total-group activity)

## MATERIALS NEEDED

- Nine strips of oak tag 2 cm × 4 cm (1 in. × 2 in.)
- Different-sized buttons and juice, soup, and soft-drink cans
- Different-colored paper (not black)
- Meter stick or yardstick

- Black marking pen
- Masking tape
- Ball of heavy string
- Long hallway (or auditorium)
- Yellow circle with 30 cm (12 in.) diameter.

## PROCEDURE

1. Tape the yellow circle to one end of the hall (or auditorium). Label it "Sun." In this model, the *sizes* of the sun and planets will not be to scale.
2. Use different-sized buttons as patterns to draw circles on colored paper to represent the smaller plants, Mercury, Venus, Earth, Mars, and Pluto.
3. Use cans of different sizes as patterns for Jupiter, Saturn, Uranus, and Neptune. Remember Jupiter and Saturn are *much* larger than the others.
4. Write the name of a planet on each of the nine strips of oak tag.
5. Tape the planet and its name in order from the sun along the wall of the hall (or auditorium) of your school. Use your meter stick to measure the following distances from the sun:

   |     |         |       |             |
   |-----|---------|-------|-------------|
   | a.  | Mercury | 39    | centimeters |
   | b.  | Venus   | 72    | centimeters |
   | c.  | Earth   | 1.00  | meter       |
   | d.  | Mars    | 1.52  | meters      |
   | e.  | Jupiter | 5.20  | meters      |
   | f.  | Saturn  | 9.52  | meters      |
   | g.  | Uranus  | 19.60 | meters      |
   | h.  | Neptune | 29.99 | meters      |
   | i.  | Pluto   | 39.37 | meters      |

   The distances were computed by using a measure called an *astronomical unit (AU)*. The distance from the earth to the sun, 149,600,000 kilometers (93,000,000 miles), is one AU. The distance of one meter has been assigned to each AU.
6. Your planets are now in rough-scale distance from the sun. Close your eyes and try to imagine how far they really are in space.

## TEACHER INFORMATION

If you use pictures of the planets drawn by the students steps 2 and 3 should be omitted. Remember, the numbers listed as decimals after the meters are centimeters. The scales and distances used in Activities 167 and 168 are only rough estimates intended to give a *feeling* of comparative size and distance.

If you do not have a long hallway or auditorium, go outdoors and measure and tape the planets to a long piece of string.

# ACTIVITY 169: How Can We Learn More about the Solar System and Space?

(Enrichment activity)

## MATERIALS NEEDED

- Library books, magazines, newspaper articles, and encyclopedias
- Filmstrips, recordings, and photos
- Drawing paper and lined paper
- Paints, crayons, and other art supplies and media

## PROCEDURE

1. Within your classroom there are books, magazines, newspaper articles, and other materials to help you learn more about the solar system and space. Find out as much as you can about one or more of the following questions and prepare a report for the class:
   a. What are comets?
   b. What are meteors?
   c. Do meteors ever strike the earth?
   d. What causes meteor showers?
   e. How big is the planet Jupiter?
   f. How does Jupiter affect other objects in the solar system (both now and in the past)?
   g. If you had to try to live on another planet or moon in the solar system, which would you choose, and why?
   h. If you wanted to become an astronaut, when, how, and where would you begin?
   i. Some animals such as coyotes and wolves are known to howl during a full moon. See if you can find stories or legends about ways the full moon is thought to affect people.
   j. Choose a special interest of your own, not listed above, and make a special study of it.

## TEACHER INFORMATION

This activity is recommended for older students trained in research skills. With younger children, it can provide an opportunity to introduce basic research methods, such as gathering, analyzing, and evaluating scientific information.

Unfortunately, new scientific discoveries are often reported on the basis of their sensational value rather than their actual contribution to the extension of scientific knowledge. This is especially true of such fields as astronomy and medicine.

There is strong scientific evidence that throughout its history the earth has regularly been struck by small and large objects from space. There is no reason to believe this will not continue. Incidents of damage or injury are extremely rare throughout recorded history.

Major areas of importance not developed in this section are the effect of tides on water, land, and atmosphere, the profound effect of Jupiter's strong gravitational field, the effect of variations in the sun's atmosphere, theories as to the origin of the solar system and universe, and the probability of the existence of other solar systems—with a real possibility of some form of life beyond the earth. These topics may suggest other areas of study or discussion for exceptionally able students.

# Bibliography

*Selected Professional Texts*

Blough, Glenn O., and Julius Schwartz. *Elementary School Science and How to Teach It* (7th ed.). New York: Holt,Rinehart & Winston, 1984.

Carin, Arthur A., and Robert B. Sund. *Teaching Science Through Discovery* (5th ed.). Columbus, Ohio: Charles E. Merrill Pub. Co., 1985.

Esler, William K., and Mary K. Esler. *Teaching Elementary Science* (4th ed.). Belmont, Calif.: Wadsworth Pub. Co., 1984.

Gega, Peter C. *Science in Elementary Education* (4th ed.). New York: John Wiley & Sons, 1982.

Jacobsen, Willard J., and Abby Barry Bergman. *Science for Children.* Englewood Cliffs, N.J.: Prentice-Hall, 1980.

Kauchak, Donald and Paul Eggen. *Exploring Science in Elementary Schools* Chicago: Rand McNally, 1980.

Rowe, Mary Budd. *Teaching Science as Continuous Inquiry: A Basic* (2 nd.). New York: McGraw-Hill, 1978.

Victor, Edward. *Science for the Elementary School* (5th ed.). New York: MacMillan Publishing Company, 1985.

*Periodicals*

*Astronomy.* Astro Media Corp., 625 E. St. Paul Ave. Milwaukee, WI 53202.
*Audubon.* National Audubon Society. 950 Third Ave., New York, NY 10022
*Discover.* Time Inc. 3435 Wilshire Blvd., Los Angeles, CA 90010
*National Geographic.* National Geographic Society, 17th and M Sts. N.W., Washington, DC 20036
*Natural History.* American Museum of Natural History, Central Park West at 79th St., New York, NY 10024
*Ranger Rick's Nature Magazine.** National Wildlife Federation, 1412 16th St. N.W., Washington, DC 20036
*Science.* American Association for the Advancement of Science, 1515 Massachusetts Ave. N.W., Washington, DC 20005
*Science and Children.* National Science Theaters Association, 1742 Connecticut Ave. N.W., Washington, DC 20009
*Smithsonian.* Smithsonian Associates, 900 Jefferson Dr., Washington, DC 20560
*World.** National Geographic Society, 17th and M Sts., Washington, DC 20036
*Zoo Books.** Wildlife Education Ltd., 930 West Washington St., San Diego, CA 92103

*For elementary age students.

Check on subscription addresses. Many periodicals are now using the National Data Center in Boulder, Colorado, rather than National Headquarters.

# Sources of Free and Inexpensive Materials for the Earth Sciences

Before requesting free and inexpensive materials, consider the following:

1. Use school stationery whenever possible. Most suppliers prefer it; some require it.
2. When requesting free materials, it is an act of courtesy to include a self-addressed, stamped envelope.
3. Do not ask for excessive amounts of free materials. Remember, the suppliers are generously paying the costs.
4. Be specific in your requests.
5. A word of thanks is in order at the time of your request and upon receipt and use of the materials.

American Iron & Steel Institute
1000 Sixteenth Street, N.W.
Washington, DC 20036
*(free booklet and filmstrip "From Supernovas to Scientists to You")*

Concern, Inc.
1794 Columbia Road, N.W.
Washington, DC 20009
*(small charge for pamphlets about ecology, water, air, wetlands, and so on)*

Forest Service
Twelfth and Independence, S.W.
P.O. Box 2417
Washington, DC 20013
*(pamphlets entitled "Suggestions for Incorporating Forestry into the School Curriculum" and "Investigating Your Environment")*

Garden Club of America
598 Madison Avenue
New York, NY 10022
*(one free "The World Around You" environmental education packet per teacher, additional copies available at a small charge)*

International Oceanographic Foundation
3979 Rickenbacker Causeway
Miami, FL 33149
*(booklets about careers in oceanography)*

National Aubudon Society
1130 Fifth Avenue
New York, NY 10001
*(catalog of materials dealing with birds, wildlife, energy, etc., with prices)*

National Coal Association
Coal Building
1130 Seventeenth Street, N.W.
Washington, DC 20036
*(publications about coal, including an activity program for grades K–3 entitled "Discovering Coal")*

National Science Teachers Association
1742 Connecticut Avenue, N.W.
Washington, DC 20009
*(catalog of science publications, posters, and other learning aids, with prices)*

Phillips Petroleum Company
Bartlesville, OK 74004
*(information about various types of energy, the energy crisis, and solutions)*

United States Department of Agriculture
Office of Information
Washington, DC 20036
*(booklets describing occupations of people on the farm)*

# Science Supply Houses

Carolina Biological Supply Co.
2700 York Rd.
Burlington, NC 27215

Central Scientific Company
2600 South Kostner Avenue
Chicago, IL 60623

Edmund Scientific
101 E. Gloucester Pike
Barrington, NJ 08007
*(Catalog for industry and education)*

Fisher Scientific Company
4901 West Lemoyne
Chicago, IL 60651

Flight Systems, Inc.
9300 East 68th Street
Raytown, MO 64133
*(Model rocketry)*

Frey Scientific
905 Hickory Lane
Mansfield, OH 44905
*(General science catalog)*

Markson Science, Inc.
7815 S. 46th St.
Phoenix, AZ 85040
*(Similar to Edmund)*

MMI Space Science Corp.
2950 Wyman Parkway
P.O. Box 19907
Baltimore, MD 21211
*(Astonomy and space science, teaching materials reference catalog)*

Sargent-Welch Scientific Co.
7300 N. Linder Ave.
P.O. Box 1026
Skokie, IL 60077
*(General science supply, similar to Frey)*

Ward's Natural Science Establishment
3000 Ridge Road East
Rochester, NY 14622